Stephen Poliakoff

Close My Eyes

Methuen Drama

A Methuen Screenplay

First published in Great Britain as a paperback original in the Methuen Screenplay series in 1991 by Methuen Drama, 81 Fulham Road, London SW3 6RB and distributed in the United States of America by HEB Inc., 361 Hanover Street, Portsmouth, New Hampshire NH 03801-3959.

Copyright © 1991 Stephen Poliakoff
The author has asserted his moral rights.

ISBN 0-413-64920-2

A CIP catalogue record for this book is available from the British Library

The front cover is taken from the poster for the film **Close My Eyes** *and shows Saskia Reeves as Natalie and Clive Owen as Richard, copyright © Film Four International, courtesy of Artificial Eye. The photographs inside the book are copyright © Film Four International, courtesy of Artificial Eye. All photos are by Simon Mein.*

Printed and bound in Great Britain
by Cox & Wyman Ltd, Cardiff Road, Reading

Preface

In 1975 I wrote a play about a brother and sister, Ralph and Clare, called *Hitting Town*. The action all took place on one winter night, during which Clare and Ralph slept together. She was recovering from being left by her lover, he from the shock of being near the Birmingham bombs when they went off.

The play was about people retreating into a private melancholy, away from the urban desolation all around them. It also tried to catch the uncertain, ugly mood of the mid-seventies, following so soon after the exuberance and confidence of the sixties.

Ever since I finished the play I've had a desire to explore the central relationship more deeply. The idea kept coming back to me over the years, troubling me. But I could not recapture those earlier characters, nor did I particularly want to. Instead of merely revisiting the play I wanted to create a new story involving a brother and sister that would reflect some of the anxieties that pursue us in the nineties.

In particular I wanted to explore sexual worries, the reality that sex is much more complicated and dangerous than it was when I wrote the original play and how that would affect one young man leading a reasonably active heterosexual life.

But the play and film do share a common purpose, a desire not to shock the audience, but to make them accept the central relationship as almost natural, for it to unfold with a beguiling momentum of its own, which discourages all moralising about it.

In 1975 *Hitting Town* inhabited a brutal concrete and neon world. *Close My Eyes* is set against a wider landscape, full of nineties *fin-de-siècle* contrasts, the rebuilding of London and the lush, prosperous, disquietingly beautiful Home Countries, during the very hot summer of 1990.

Both stories show characters trying to escape from the present and, in Richard's case in *Close My Eyes*, very nearly succeeding. The present in *Hitting Town* was a dirty, lonely, plastic and hideous place. In *Close My Eyes* it is more seductive, especially during this unbelievably hot summer, but it is also a lot more dangerous.

Stephen Poliakoff
June 1991

Close My Eyes opened in the UK on 6 September 1991
with the following cast:

Sinclair	Alan Rickman
Richard	Clive Owen
Natalie	Saskia Reeves
Colin	Karl Johnson
Jessica	Lesley Sharp
Paula	Kate Gartside
Philippa	Karen Knight
Geal	Niall Buggy
Scotsman	Campbell Morrison
Stoney-Faced Woman	Annie Hayes
Balding Man	Maxwell Hutcheon
Dark Haired Girl	Geraldine Somerville
Scottish Girl	Helen FitzGerald
Noley	Christopher Barr
Hotel Porter	Gordon Salkilld
Maid	Choy Ling Man
Pimply Young Man	John Albasiny
Selina	Marie Passarelli
Doreen	Jan Winters

Directed by Stephen Poliakoff
Produced by Therese Pickard
Music by Michael Gibbs
Director of Photography Witold Stok
Production Designer Luciana Arrighi

A Beambright Production for Film Four International
released by Artificial Eye.

Interior: **Natalie**'s *room: Night:*

The camera moves through a modern room, in a small but quite elegant flat, towards the figure of **Natalie** *who is standing in a thin summer dress with her back to us.*

We pass some candles, beginning to burn low, records strewn around, one playing loudly on a battered gramophone. The camera passes an old ornamental oil lamp on a modern table and without a cut we move with **Natalie** *onto the balcony into the night air, where a spread of glittering city lights falls away below us.*

The area is surrounded by tall modern flats. **Natalie** *stares down to the concourse below as if waiting for someone.*

Natalie *is in her late twenties at the start of the action. There is a musky, hot atmosphere as she waits, the candles burning round her, and the music playing.*

Exterior: City streets: Credit sequence: Night:

Below us we see a figure approaching, very small at first, seen from a great height, as the credits play.

We cut to the figure of **Richard** *and track with him along the concourse past an eerily empty landscape of wide walkways and bridges, across night roads. But the atmosphere is not desolate, the night lights, the music and the lettering of the credits make it seem velvety and expectant.*

Interior: Staircase: Night:

We watch, under the final credits, the figure of **Richard** *weave his way up the staircase towards us, seen from a great height.* **Natalie**, *leaning over the bannister.* **Richard** *running up floor after floor without apparent effort.*

A caption comes up – '1985' – as we stare down into the stairwell.

Natalie (*calling*) You're late.

Richard Sorry, it was unavoidable. Trains on Sunday . . . you know what they're like.

Natalie Unavoidable – I don't believe it. I've eaten all the food.

Richard (*grins*) You've eaten all the food? Now that's serious. (*He looks at her.*) Aren't you pleased to see me?

Natalie (*lightly*) NO!

Interior: **Natalie**'s *room: Night:*

Cut to a wide shot of the two. **Natalie** *lighting a couple more candles.* **Richard** *sitting on the floor, scraping the last traces of food out of a bowl.*

Richard Is this all there is?

Natalie I told you.

Richard (*glancing round*) What are all the candles for anyway? – it's spooky. (*He grins.*) Is this what you used to get up to with him every night?

Natalie I just like it – that's all.

Richard (*lightly*) You've got to stop it. It looks like you're grieving – grieving for a relationship! Must make it ten times worse.

Natalie Thank you Richard, I've been waiting here for the last six hours just to hear you say that. It is all I need.

Richard (*licking bowl*) It *is* what you need. (*Moving.*) Come on, I'm going to get you out of here, this place is bad for you.

Natalie No, there's nowhere to go round here on a Sunday.

Richard (*affectionate smile*) Now she can't go out of the house! – come on Natalie, there's no need to over-do it!

Natalie's *pale worried face looking at him.*

Exterior: The concourse: Night:

Cut to **Natalie** *and* **Richard** *moving through the night landscapes.* **Natalie** *has put on an old fur coat over her light red summer dress.* **Richard** *tugging her on.* **Natalie** *stops to light a cigarette.*

Richard (*disbelieving*) She can't even get down the street without one! (*He tugs her on.*)

Interior: Restaurant: Night:

A long thin Wimpy-style restaurant with ceiling fans going round in the hot night air, a half-hearted mural along the wall, and most of the restaurant in semi-darkness. **Richard** *and* **Natalie** *are sitting in the shadows below the mural, far away from a couple of waitresses standing together by the counter in a pool of white light.*

Richard Can you believe this! They boast of a waitress service and then they take no notice of you. (*He calls out.*) Excuse me . . .

Natalie It's OK. You've got me out of the flat. (*Lightly.*) We can just sit here and enjoy the decor.

Richard (*looking at the mouldy fur coat*) Why are you wearing that?

Natalie *moves back in her seat.*

Richard I don't like seeing you unhappy.

Natalie Well, I am unhappy. (*Self-mocking smile.*) I'm incredibly unhappy – I mean you buy a flat with your lover and then he leaves you within two months. Six and a half weeks, actually! Not many worse things.

Richard No.

Natalie And now Mum and Dad have both gone – you are the only person I can tell (*She begins to laugh.*) which is terrible!

They both laugh.

Natalie (*looking at him*) I haven't seen you for ages.

Richard (*who is unscrewing the top of the mustard, peering in*) I'm sorry, I've been very busy.

Natalie Students aren't busy. (*Poking him gently.*)

Richard (*charming smile*) It's a good course planning pretend cities . . . I'm very happy.

Natalie I bet you are, plenty of girls.

Richard Absolutely.

Natalie Endless time to lie around and talk, (*With a trace of envy.*) raving it up in London.

Richard *has picked up the plastic red tomato and put it on his plate.*

Stop playing with those. What are you doing?

Richard (*unscrewing top of tomato*) You should always look in these wherever you go – can judge a town by what's in its tomato.

Natalie (*lightly*) Stop it – that's disgusting.

Richard (*pulling out of tomato*) What have we got? Not a bad catch . . . some chewing gum, a few coins . . . and what's this . . . A tooth! Natalie, somebody's popped a tooth in here.

Natalie (*horrified but really laughing*) Jesus – I am never using those things again. EVER!

Exterior: City: Night:

Cut to a shot of **Richard** *and* **Natalie** *alone in the city, crossing a square at night, seen from a great height.* **Richard** *is moving ahead of her.*

Richard Come on, Natalie . . . you're out of condition. Take the coat off, for goodness' sake, it's so warm. (*The coat coming off in a swirling movement,* **Natalie** *in the red dress running, trying to catch him up.*) . . . too much smoking . . . look at you . . . Come on!

Interior: Bedroom: Night:

They move into a room with two bunk beds for children and a mobile brushing them in the middle of the room. Wallpaper showing elephants in brightly coloured hot air balloons.

Natalie Come on, you can sleep in here.

Richard (*laughs*) Kids' beds – you were already planning for two kids. (*Lightly.*) No wonder he left – fled in terror!

Natalie (*slight laugh, playfully nudging him*) Stop it! No, we bought it like this – we were just going to have them removed.

Richard (*touching the thin walls*) Not too bad, this flat, but the finish is cheap . . . It's not built with love.

Close-up of **Natalie**, *looking vulnerable, musak playing.* **Richard** *notices a little pile of belongings in the corner, large men's shoes left behind.*

Natalie (*looking up at him, indicating the pounding music from next door*) It's not usually as loud as this. He must have known you were coming.

Interior: Bedroom: Middle of the night:

Cut to **Richard** *lying in bed, his eyes flick open. Music still playing, a dull, audible pounding. Clock ticking by his bed showing it's 3.30.*

Richard Jesus!

He gets up, in underpants. He pulls a shirt round his shoulders.

Interior: Main room: Night:

Richard *moves angrily into the main part of the flat. Music is still very audible. He suddenly sees* **Natalie** *lying in the shadows, a large glass pudding dish full of water beside her. She's floating small, lighted candles on the water.*

Richard *kneels beside her hunched shape on the floor, the lighted bowl between them.*

Natalie Oh Richard . . . make it better! I wish I could wake up and be *happy*! Just one morning, it would be gone, this feeling, and never come back.

Richard, *nonchalantly playing with her lovely thirties necklace.*

Richard You can make that happen, get out of town, start all over again.

Natalie A new career? I'm too old to start again.

Richard You're not too old! Don't be stupid. That job was never what you wanted – a buyer for that bloody awful store, you wanted to be *artistic*.

Natalie But I'm not artistic.

Richard (*smiles*) But you want to be.

Natalie (*turns her head, looking very vulnerable*) Kiss me . . .

Richard *kisses her, a brotherly kiss. She suddenly hugs and kisses*

him with surprising intensity, pulling him so close, so tight.
Richard *pulls away, slightly taken aback by the intensity in her eyes.*

Natalie Sorry – I just needed something to hug. Even you . . . (*She smiles.*) Even my little brother. (*She moves away in the shadows.*) Go back to sleep. And you haven't made me feel better, so don't look so smug.

Interior: Main room: Early morning:

We see the empty room in the early morning sun, sweet papers, chocolates, and ashtrays strewn round where **Natalie** *had been lying in the little nest on the floor, the candles all out.*

Interior: Passage/staircase: Day:

Cut to **Richard** *emerging in shirt, jeans, barefoot, carrying one of the large shoes, moving along the passage towards the door from which the music is* still *pounding. He wallops the door with the shoe.*

Richard Switch it off, you moron, for Chrissake! (*Thumping door.*) Go on.

Natalie *rushes out after him, restraining him.*

Natalie Stop it, Richard! Stop it. (*Laughing.*) I've never seen the guy, he might kill us! Come on.

They move off down the passage towards where the sun is splashing down the staircase from the next floor.

Exterior: Roof: Day:

We cut to them emerging onto the roof, surveying the view. Tall buildings jutting up behind them, dwarfing them. **Richard** *moving around the ducts on the roof.*

Natalie Where are you going?

Richard Getting away from that music. (*Touching the thirties necklace.*) You have *definitely* got to leave here.

Natalie OK. OK.

Richard I mean it. (*Quiet smile.*) You could do anything if you set your mind to it.

Natalie That's not true. (*Looking at him.*) *You* are always so confident, Richard.

Richard (*suddenly exclaiming and pointing*) Look, look! Look at this!

Natalie *looks down horrified. Out of a crack in the roof several giant cockroaches are happily marching around.*

Natalie (*appalled smile*) Oh my God!

Richard I told you about this building, didn't I? Now you've *got* to leave. You ought to come and join me in London. Oh yes.

They are moving away from the cockroaches.

Natalie Jesus, they're following us! *They are!*

Richard (*laughing*) You see, no choice now!

They are hopping around among the cockroaches on the roof.

Exterior: Kings Cross Station: Day:

We cut to a pan down from large advertisements of escapist images, beaches or mountains, high up on the walls of Kings Cross Station, to find **Richard** *strolling nonchalantly along the concourse, he is smartly and expensively dressed, and pulling an elegant little luggage trolley of an unusual design.*

A caption comes up: 'Two Years Later'. **Richard** *stops in the middle of the station, he feels in his inside pocket, mumbles to himself, shakes his head.*

Richard Shit.

Interior: Office: Day:

Cut to heavily designed office, full of plants, mid-eighties chic, very young men and women sheltering among the plants and computers. **Natalie**, *the oldest person there, is sitting typing on a word processor when she picks up the phone. She is trying to look chic in this atmosphere but is obviously ill at ease. She has to share a table with another girl.*

Intercut with:

Interior: Phone booth: Kings Cross Station: Day:

Richard *in phone booth at Kings Cross.*

Richard It is me.

Natalie What's the matter?

Richard I've left my wallet at your flat.

Natalie So go and fetch it.

Richard I haven't got a key! Please . . . they've announced the train!

Natalie I don't believe this, you appear out of nowhere, use my flat as a hotel, I hardly see you and –

Richard Natalie . . . just this time, please.

Interior: **Natalie***'s Office: Day:*

A **Dark Haired Girl**, *who is no more than 22, is talking to an older secretary.*

Dark Haired Girl Look, how many times do I have to tell you, I don't want it done like this – you really disappoint me, Alice, when you don't *listen*.

Natalie (*to phone, staring at girl*) I'll have to get permission . . . have to ask my 14-year-old boss.

Natalie *stares with apprehension towards the* **Girl**.

Exterior: Kings Cross: Day:

Natalie *appears on walkway above platform.* **Richard** *sees her across the concourse. They meet on the platform among a maze of empty, blue trolleys.*

Natalie (*handing wallet*) There! The things I do for you, I can't believe it.

Richard (*grinning*) I can . . . I'll pay you back sometime.

Natalie (*indicating* **Richard***'s luggage trolley*) And what is that? I've never seen a trolley like this.

Richard It's Swedish – a new design. It's great, isn't it?

Natalie (*laughing*) Trust you to have one, and (*Picking up lunch box.*) a cordon bleu packed lunch!

Richard Naturally! (*Whistle blows, he glances round, then back.*) How's the job?

Natalie Now he asks! It's horrible there. I've become a *secretary*. My boss is terrifying, I'm going backwards.

Whistle blows, both heads move.

I look for somewhere trendy to work, 'creative', and see what happens. I feel like I'm 150 – *and* six years old!

Richard (*reproachfully*) Stop it.

Natalie OK, OK, yes. I can do anything – you told me. (*She smiles.*) So it must be true. You're not listening.

Richard (*looks towards platform, whistle blowing*) It's just . . . no, it should be OK.

Natalie I've been meaning to talk to you – and now I try to do it here!

They look at each other, a tense, strained moment, **Richard** *wanting to go but not wishing to seem callous.*

Natalie This is stupid! Go on then, GO.

Richard *hesitates.*

GO.

Richard It's just the train . . . (*Gives her a little peck of a kiss.*) 'Bye.

He moves off purposefully.

Natalie You'd better write, or I'll kill you. And ring too. Scotland's not that far away.

Richard (*calling back*) I may be busy!

Natalie (*calling*) No, you won't. Building a new town, that's nothing. You'll have plenty of time!

Richard *falls into step with a tall blonde, helps her with her luggage.* **Natalie** *watching him disappear with the girl, then realises she's holding the special packed lunch. She smiles to herself, walks off with it, swinging it as she walks.*

Interior: Empty office and passage: Day:

A phone ringing somewhere, as the camera moves through a new empty open-plan office towards a glass partition. Everything is still wrapped in paper and plastic sheets, whole building still in cotton wool. As the camera moves we hear giggles and laughter. A caption on the screen: 'One Year Later'.

Interior: Old office: Day:

Close-up of **Natalie** *on telephone wiping her nose, she has a streaming cold. She looks puffy and harrassed.*

Natalie (*on phone*) Come on . . . where are you?

We see in a wide shot she is in a large almost Dickensian office with heavy mahogany desk, tall windows, huge dusty files. It is grey outside, a dismal rainy atmosphere. Opposite her a **Pimply Young Man** *is giving her knowing smiles. He has a large blotter in front of him and is making a series of patterns out of coffee stains, rings from the bottom of his coffee cup.*

Natalie (*more urgent*) Richard, be there.

Interior: Modern office: Day:

We cut back to the modern office. The camera moves through the glass partition. Then a bare arm suddenly shoots up and answers the phone. **Richard**'s *face appears slightly sweaty, broad grin.*

Richard Hello . . . Natalie! It's you!

Wide shot, we see he is naked with a **Scottish Girl** *in the middle of an empty office where everything is still covered in plastic sheeting.* **Richard** *moves very relaxed, naked with the phone, as he talks, warm in the air-conditioned office.*

Intercut with:

Interior: Old office: Day:

The very draughty office **Natalie** *is in.*

Natalie Richard – what's the matter?

Richard Nothing . . . I was busy.

The **Scottish Girl** *gets up naked, beginning unhurriedly to put on her clothes.*

Richard (*to her*) It's only my sister.

Natalie Only! Who's that you are talking to?

Richard (*lightly*) My secretary. We're all alone here.

Natalie What are you giggling for? (*Suddenly.*) I suppose you were in the middle of screwing her.

Eyes flash all around **Natalie** *in the silent office.*

Richard As it happens, yes. But this is not a regular occurrence. (*He watches the* **Scottish Girl** *put on her jeans.*)

Natalie Jesus – I'm ringing off. You're incorrigible, it's 4 o'clock in the afternoon.

Natalie *stares down at a revolting cup of milky tea on her desk. The* **Pimply Young Man** *is watching her.*

We cut to **Richard**.

Richard (*relaxed and naked*) We're celebrating our last days of freedom. They've finally got the office finished. People will be moving in . . . (*Watching the* **Scottish Girl**.) It's going to get a lot more formal here.

Natalie (*staring about her*) I'm so cold, Richard, it's dismal here.

Richard The one thing we've got is marvellous central heating.

Natalie (*angry*) You're meant to be cold in Scotland!

Cut back to the **Scottish Girl**, *standing bare-backed by the* *window in her jeans, letting her hair blow in the air from the heater.*

Richard (*gently*) I know.

Natalie I thought I needed a drastic change. I've got my own desk! But the place is like out of a horror movie, it was out of date before the war. (*Staring at files.*)

Richard Maybe it's time to move on again.

Natalie You always make it sound so easy.

Richard Well, *I've* got a new job.

Natalie Another one!

Richard This one is on the continent . . . if I get it.

Natalie (*real alarm in her eyes*) What, you mean? You'll be going abroad?

Richard Maybe. Yes.

Close-up of **Natalie**.

Look, I've got to put some clothes on, (*Gently.*) I'll call you tomorrow, I promise.

Natalie (*furious*) Yes, it might be an idea to get dressed, wandering about naked in the middle of your office, that's ridiculous. I don't like this conversation. (*She slams down the phone.*)

Interior: Modern office: Day:

Cut back to **Richard**'s *office, he is pouring wine into paper cups. The* **Scottish Girl** *sitting opposite him. They are both now dressed in shirts and jeans.*

Scottish Girl I didn't know you were going abroad.

Richard (*warm smile*) Yes – it's a big job, Pan-European, integrated transport planning, and other buzz words. I never thought I'd get it.

Scottish Girl (*letting the heater blow her hair, moving her head from side to side*) You get jobs very easily, don't you.

Richard (*self-mocking smile*) Yes, I don't know why that is . . . maybe other people forget to apply.

Scottish Girl (*teasing smile*) Means I can try for your job, can't I. (*Sensual smile.*) Let's have another little celebration, shall we?

We stay on her head, her hair blowing in the draught from the heater, a warm relaxed moment.

Interior: The old office: Day:

Natalie *now alone in the grey office, with just the* **Pimply Young Man**, *who is making another coffee ring on the blotter, and smiling at her, in a slightly predatory fashion.*

Natalie *starts feverishly circling new jobs in the 'Jobs Vacant' section of a newspaper. The* **Pimply Young Man** *staring at her, giving her little knowing smiles.*

Natalie *heaves and pushes the heavy desk away, so she can get out from behind it and escape. A desolate image with the rain on the windows.*

Exterior: London: Day:

Cut to wide shots of London. Canary Wharf, ghostly, growing in the early morning light, massive structure climbing into the sky. The river, and the changing landscape, new development sprouting around the river. In the shadow of these a large old warehouse building, unconverted, walls still grey. The camera peers down at it from a great height. A caption on the image says 'Two Years Later'.

Interior: 'Urban Alert' offices: Day:

Large high-walled interior with flaking plaster dominated by the peeling decorative crest of the merchant company that once owned the warehouse, on the wall. The interior is divided into loosely planned office space, with rough and ready partitions. And there is a wide passage with tall quite elegant windows leading towards some large ancient service lifts.

Through the Venetian blinds covering the glass of one of the partitioned offices, **Jessica***, a woman in her late twenties, is staring into the passage. She can see* **Richard** *sitting waiting there, in a fine suit, looking sleeker, slightly older, successful. Sun splashing the passage, dust visible in the sun.* **Colin***, a very pale thin-faced man in his thirties joins* **Jessica** *by the blinds.*

Colin Is that him?

Jessica It must be.

Colin I don't like the look of him at all. (*Sharp smile.*) Let's keep him waiting.

Cut back to **Richard***, his arms stretched out along wall as he sits, looking elegant and coolly detached.*

Interior: **Colin***'s office: Day:*

Cut to **Colin** *in mid-sentence, interviewing* **Richard** *in his cramped office, spilling over with files, but they are neatly stacked, and there is a computer on the desk.* **Colin** *is sitting on the window sill, and* **Richard** *on a very low seat, so he has to stare up at him.*

Colin Frankly, I'm amazed to see somebody like you here.

The salary cut you'd be taking is immense, I mean all these jobs you've done, Pan-European, Brussels . . .

Richard Yes, take no notice of that. I've always for some reason been very good at landing terrific jobs . . .

Colin *stares at him coldly.*

. . . without having the right qualifications for them. It was just luck. And I wasn't happy doing them.

Colin So you think you're going to get this job do you?

Richard Not at the moment, no.

Colin You mean you only get *terrific* jobs and this isn't one of them.

Richard No, I meant this interview is going rather badly so . . . (*He pulls out a cigarette.*) I don't smoke, I just fiddle with them.

Jessica *looking through window.*

I've changed you see, I saw there was more to life than planning new roads, (*Self-mocking smile.*) I discovered the 'environment', a bit late maybe . . . I'm not putting this well. I've seen so much incompetence among developers . . . bad planning – I want to do something about that.

Colin (*staring straight at him*) You realise we have no money to speak of, we get *some* funds from the local council. There are no planning controls in this part of town, all we can do is *hound*.

Richard (*smiles*) A sort of urban Greenpeace . . .

A shot of **Jessica** *watching outside the office. Cut back to* **Colin**.

Colin (*cold stare*) It might be useful to have a professional town planner, who'd respond really quickly with alternative plans to any situation.

Richard That's right. (*Very slight pause.*)

Colin (*briskly*) I'll let you know. I'll call you.

Richard No. You tell me now.

Colin's *eyes narrow.*

Richard I prefer to cut the bullshit. And I imagine you do too.

Colin's *arm suddenly goes up, plucks a file from above his head and chucks it down at* **Richard** *so it lands with a thud in his stomach.*

Colin We have a meeting with Lappenshaw Mercantile at the end of the week, we're only 'granted' face to face meetings very occasionally, it's a chance for us.

Richard (*taking the file*) Great.

Richard *getting up,* **Colin** *watching him.*

Colin We may look like a bunch of ex-hippies but I fire people at a moment's notice. You ought to know that. It's much worse here than at a merchant bank.

Interior: 'Urban Alert' offices: **Richard**'s *office: Day:*

High shot, mid-afternoon light, the camera moving across the office, phones are ringing, people working hard, we see **Richard** *in his office, behind a makeshift partition. He has covered the walls with an eclectic collection of posters, some nostalgic, some very urban and modern. He is pacing up and down, reading a file, with paper chaotically spread all around him.*

Jessica *pushes back books on top of partition, speaks through the gap.*

Jessica Phone call for you.

Richard I can't take it.

Jessica It's your sister.

Richard (*off hand*) Oh shit, yes, I was meant to . . . I suppose I better take it.

Interior: **Natalie**'s *bedroom: Day:*

Natalie *in profile, lying on her bed, just her face in semi-darkness, and the afternoon light through the bedroom window.*

Intercut with:

Interior: **Richard**'s *office: Day:*

Richard I've been really busy, I'm sorry, I've been meaning . . .

Natalie You've been back six weeks – you haven't called.

Richard (*not concentrating, looking at file*) I did call! I left a message on your machine.

Natalie Took till yesterday! (*Her face in shadow.*) You want to come over and meet Sinclair?

Richard Who?

Natalie Don't do that . . . *Sinclair.* Since you didn't manage to make it to the wedding.

As **Richard** *is on the phone,* **Jessica** *calls out.*

Jessica (*calling at him*) Food! Food's up!

Richard *looks up, a very pretty girl,* **Paula**, *in some sort of restaurant uniform, is handing out take-away food boxes dropping them on desks.*

Richard (*on phone, very abstracted*) Sure . . . Yeah . . . why not. Lunch on Saturday, fine. I'll try to make it. (*He replaces the receiver, looks at* **Jessica**.) Families!

Interior: **Natalie**'s *bedroom: Day:*

We settle for a second back on **Natalie**'s *face in semi-darkness, lying on pillow, her eyes staring out.*

Interior: **Richard**'s *office: Day:*

Jessica (*watching* **Paula** *with food*) He may work us hard, but Colin does send out for great take-aways.

Richard (*staring at* **Paula** *as she comes towards him*) So I see.

We cut to **Colin** *and* **Jessica** *staring at* **Richard** *as he chats up* **Paula** *among the piles and piles of paper in his office.*

Colin (*watching* **Richard** *flirt with* **Paula**) I'm beginning to think we've made a real mistake.

Interior: **Natalie**'s *kitchen: Day:*

Cut to ingredients being laid out as if for an operation, spotless utensils, magnificent ingredients, for the making of a summer pudding.

Interior: Developer's office and passage: Day:

Colin, **Jessica**, **Richard** *and a couple of others from the office walking towards us down a plush passage. Then we see their approach being watched through an open door by* **Geal** *and three other city types sitting behind a desk.*

Geal (*watching their approach*) What a miserable looking bunch.

Richard *staring at* **Geal** *as they approach through door, into the* *room with its blinds drawn against the sun, gold and black light, half-light.*

Richard It looks like they've modelled themselves on those banking commercials on TV.

They sit opposite each other. The businessmen the same age or slightly younger than the pressure group.

Geal Delighted to see you all here. I'm sure you're going to give us a clean bill of health.

Interior: **Natalie**'*s kitchen: Day:*

We see food being prepared, fruit, meringues, and especially a summer pudding being finished, the blackcurrants gleaming, the pudding a rich dark red. **Natalie**, *cooking on her own, licking the juice from the pudding off her fingers.*

Interior: Developers' building: Day:

Cut back to **Colin** *awkwardly in the middle of a speech to the businessmen, stuttering, realising he's not having impact.*

Colin . . . However many times you say that, the fact is you said there'd be access to Threepenny Street . . . and . . . and an open space there, and there.

Geal I think you will find we have done everything we stated we would – there is not a single public statement, or a single promise that we've made, which we've failed to honour. If there is, I'd be interested to see what it is!

Colin But that is not the case, your wording was ambiguous, maybe, but everybody took it to mean . . . (*His papers suddenly fluttering everywhere scattering across desk and room.*)

Noley (*sidekick to* **Geal**, *slightly older, watching* **Colin** *with great contempt*) Want any help with those?

Interior: **Natalie**'s *kitchen: Day:*

Cut back to **Natalie**'s *kitchen, the bread soaking in the blackcurrant juice, the pudding being moulded into shape by delicate fingers, more dark juice being poured over it, and more fruit squeezed inside it, fresh raspberries and blackcurrants.*

Interior: Developers' office: Day:

Geal Gentlemen, (*Correcting himself.*) and to the lady present, I don't want to seem impatient – but we are under no obligation to see you, and it is Saturday, we have now spent fifty minutes, and I think nobody would quarrel with that. You have not been able to show us one instant –

Richard Just one moment.

Richard *gets up and opens the door, they all stare at him surprised.*

Geal (*smiles*) You leaving us?

In the passage two **Security Guards** *look up in surprise.*

Richard Exactly what has happened here?

Geal (*grinning*) What do you mean?

Richard This passage, the guards.

Geal Our security system. (*To the others.*) Your friend is not making himself clear.

Richard (*suddenly producing a piece of paper from back pocket*) You know you said on August 4th, 'Our new block will be an asset for the whole area, we want to share it'.

Geal Exactly.

Richard 'We are proud of it, and as is the regular practice in America, the public will be allowed to see the full glories of our foyer at any time, and there will be public tours of the building every day of the week.' (*He smiles.*) But getting in here, Mr Geal, is more difficult than entering Fort Knox – this promise was crap, wasn't it?

Geal I'm not aware of having made this statement, but it is a small matter . . .

Richard (*producing another piece of paper*) Absolutely, and talking of small matters, let us now move on to the matter of Threepenny Street. On September 3rd in a speech you made . . .

Shot of **Geal** *looking discomfited.*

Interior: **Natalie***'s kitchen: Day:*

Cut to the pudding reaching its climax, its completion.

Exterior: Canary Wharf: Day:

Cut to the group moving along the road by the river, the vast building works behind them, towering above.

Richard *is walking slightly behind the group.* **Colin** *still formidably aloof, the others obviously impressed with* **Richard***.*

Jessica (*coming up to him*) Well done.

Richard Yes, well Colin doesn't look too pleased.

Jessica (*she smiles*) What do you expect, applause from him!

Richard (*suddenly stops*) Shit, I was meant to go to lunch with my sister, Jesus!

Smoke blowing from road works.

It's too late now. Forget it! She's married some boring guy. I was meant to meet him.

Richard *moving into smoke, stops dead again.*

Jessica (*staring at him amazed*) Why don't you go?

Richard I better go, hadn't I?

Exterior: Surrey approach: Day:

Cut to the voluptuous views of Surrey, the Thames Valley, the large houses sheltering behind thick foliage, exotic, rich shots, Surrey seen as surprisingly, almost disturbingly lush, and large vistas almost un-English in their size and contrast. The shots starting high and distant and closing in on **Richard** *driving an old open-topped Triumph Herald, but well kept, moving along the sleepy streets. The car slowing, as we see houses, surrounded by clusters of roses, and the car stops completely as* **Natalie** *and* **Sinclair**'s *house slips into view, imposing red brick Edwardian house with a huge conservatory and a tower.*

Exterior: The house: Day:

Cut to **Richard** *on foot now, moving up the path, glancing at the garden packed with flowers, it is heavy with colour and scent.*

He rings the bell and the door opens a second later and **Natalie** *is standing there. A vitally important shot: her face moves out of the half shadow, slowly glimpsed as the door opens.*

She looks stunning. Her hair is different. Her eyes alive. She is beautifully dressed. For a moment **Richard** *stares at her in surprise.*

Natalie You are unbelievably late.

Richard (*very quiet*) I know.

Natalie There is practically no food left.

Richard (*amused, remembering*) I've eaten all the food.

Natalie What?

Richard Don't you remember? (*He looks into her eyes.*) Nothing? This house, Natalie . . . it's extraordinary. I thought I'd come to the wrong place.

Natalie Are you going to come in – or are you going to admire it from out there?

Interior: The conservatory: Day:

We cut to a group sitting around a round table in the massive conservatory. A vine climbs up the conservatory walls with grapes hanging ripely all around. There are other plants and flowers, late afternoon hazy summer light. This is our first sight of **Sinclair***, a dynamic sharp-faced man, full of energy, quick-witted eyes, warm chuckling laugh. He is sitting commandingly at the centre of the group, next to* **Philippa***, a woman in her early twenties, with two golden-haired girls sitting near her, all of them in expensive summer clothes, a young man by her, and two other handsome women, lying in a post-prandial lazy way, the remnants of a gorgeous meal spread on the table.*

Sinclair The brother! This, at last, must be the brother.

Richard (*he smiles*) Yes, at last, it is.

Sinclair (*pointing at summer pudding*) I've been eyeing this last portion wondering if I could possibly eat it. (*Warm smile.*) But now you've turned up! . . . sit, sit . . . have some cold soup.

Sinclair *ladles the soup out.* **Richard** *is glancing round at the other women, the golden-haired children and* **Natalie** *moving in the conservatory. He keeps glancing back at her, taking another look.*

Sinclair It's all your fault we have eaten so much. (*He stares at* **Richard**, *a warm but shrewd look.*) I've heard so much about you – most of it extremely interesting.

Philippa (*a warm smile*) It's lovely to meet you.

Something plops from the ceiling of the conservatory into **Richard**'s *soup.*

Sinclair (*smiles*) Take no notice of that, it adds to the flavour.

Richard (*looking about him at the profusion of flowers and foliage*) This is amazing, this place – it's like a grotto or something.

Sinclair You've seen nothing yet.

Exterior: Garden by river: Day:

Sinclair *moving along the lawn overlooking the river, imposing houses on the other side, one of them with palm trees.* **Philippa**, *the children, and* **Natalie**, *moving behind them across the grass.*

Sinclair This is the 'estate'.

Richard Very impressive.

Sinclair I love it here. (*Staring across the water.*) I thought when we moved here we'd stand out, eccentrics amongst all these rich pricks, but not a bit of it, the place is full of madmen, dreamers, psychopaths, (*Waving at the houses across the water.*) bank managers who want to be painters, deep-freeze merchants who want to be poets. We're really rather boringly normal and restrained in comparison.

Natalie *is moving among the flowers,* **Richard** *watching her out of the corner of his eye, fascinated by the change in her appearance.*

Sinclair (*suddenly up to him*) I see you are reading the guilt-book!

Richard (*startled*) What?

Sinclair (*plucking book from* **Richard**'s *jacket pocket*) Proust . . . Volume 7, or is that just for our benefit? If you carry that around people automatically think – 'Jesus, I feel so *guilty*. I've never read it'. Proust! I'm afraid, though it's nauseating to admit it, I've read the entire book in French.

Richard I've read some in French.

Sinclair You're very good at languages, I hear. (*Smiles at* **Richard** *and breaks into Spanish*.) Mi burro favorito vive en Salamanca. ¿Ha estado ustéd allí?

Richard No conozco bien España.

Sinclair (*changes immediately into Italian*) La prossima volta che vieni a Verona invita mi a prendere il te. (*A sudden burst of Dutch*.) Mign vriend Herman van der Horst hasst zojuist een nieuw supermarket complex ge-opened.

The strength of his personality is overwhelming, but it's also warm and funny.

Sinclair That's Dutch – an amazingly ugly language – how about Norwegian – (*He bursts into Norwegian*.) Har du vaert i den del av skogen før. Actually, I'm not fluent in Norwegian. I have to admit.

Natalie (*quiet*) Stop showing off Sinclair . . . please.

Sinclair Rubbish, he's enjoying it. (*He begins to move off*.)

Natalie (*slight laugh*) Apart from anything else, it makes me feel so ignorant.

Sinclair (*heading off*) He must see the car. (*Charming smile*.) You want to see the car, don't you?

Exterior: Garage: Day:

Cut to the garage door opening, slowly going up as they watch.

Richard It's not a Rolls I hope.

A beautiful vintage Bentley is revealed, shining in the darkness.

Sinclair Very predictable I know, and it's very vulgar showing it to people, but it's a magnificent car. (*Charming smile.*) I just can't help it!

Richard *watching* **Natalie** *who has moved nearer the car.*

Natalie He doesn't let me drive it.

Sinclair Nobody drives it – we've got other cars for that. I do believe, I have to confess, in spending money, not just hoarding it.

Richard (*amused*) Of course.

Sinclair And fortunately there's a lot of money in being able to tell people what's going to happen! Business trends, analysis. The wonderful thing is you can make an awful lot even if you're wrong. Most people don't realise that. (*Shrewd look.*) But I'm not wrong. Not often. (*He moves off.*) Come on Nats, tea time.

Natalie Oh no, Sinclair, not more eating. What about your diet?

Sinclair The diet starts tomorrow. Tea is definitely overdue.

Interior: Boathouse: Day:

Natalie *staring at* **Richard** *in the boathouse, a moment between them, alone together.*

Natalie (*quiet*) So what do you think!

Richard (*looking round*) Oh, it's . . . amazing, and everything is wonderful.

Natalie And Sinclair?

Richard Oh he's . . . great. Does he ever stop talking?

Natalie (*smiles*) Not when he's eating – as you will see.

Richard Does he ever let you say anything?

Natalie Oh yes, of course. (*Slight smile.*) Once a week, at least.

Richard (*imitating her new Home Counties voice*) And how did you get to speak like this?

Natalie (*self-mocking smile, exaggerating her new voice*) I've always spoken like this, haven't I?

Natalie *is wearing the same thirties necklace as when he saw her at the beginning of the film. Involuntarily he reaches out and touches it.*

Richard Why are you wearing this?

Natalie What do you mean, why?

Richard You wore it that night when I visited you in your flat. You remember . . .

Natalie (*looking at necklace*) I don't think so.

Richard You look all . . . all . . . (*Embarrassed smile.*)

Natalie (*staring at him*) All what?

Richard (*laughs*) All different. I wasn't expecting –

Natalie I know you weren't.

Sinclair *comes in.*

Sinclair A brother and sister reunion. I intrude. (*He smiles.*) I'll withdraw. (*Suddenly to* **Richard**.) But you'd forgotten it was her birthday hadn't you? Nat's birthday.

Richard *surprised. He has forgotten.*

Interior: Conservatory: Early evening:

Natalie *blowing out the candles on cake.*

Sinclair (*ebullient, the force of his personality, he catches hold of* **Natalie***'s arm*) Not like that! Blow them out separately, one by one.

Natalie *hesitates.*

Sinclair No, go on darling, do it, a wish for *each one*. What are you waiting for? *Go on.*

Natalie *begins blowing them out separately, embarrassed in front of everyone.* **Richard** *watching her, their eyes meet over the cake.* **Natalie** *blowing out the candles.*

Sinclair (*as this is happening, with cream dispenser*) You see this is a new sort of cream dispenser – market research showed people hated cream coming out of tubes, like toothpaste, so they've made this cow – it's meant to be an elegant cow.

Philippa *laughing at him.*

Go on, squeeze its udders, go on . . .

Natalie *is still blowing out the candles.* **Sinclair** *notices her again.*

Sinclair Come on darling, haven't you finished yet!

Natalie *blows out the last one.* **Sinclair** *hands her the knife.*

Sinclair That took long enough. Anybody would think you'd never done it before!

We stay on **Natalie** *looking embarrassed and vulnerable.*

Exterior: Field near the house: Evening:

Natalie *and* **Richard** *walking in a field dotted with flowers.* **Sinclair** *walking a little behind, wearing a floppy hat. The gnats chasing each other in the evening air.* **Natalie** *plucking the tops off the long grass as she walks. A particularly fine view from the field across the river.*

Richard I never realised the Home Counties were so beautiful. All this so near the City.

Sinclair Yes, all sorts of things happened here. It was the site of a great Victorian party at the end of the last century. They had columns of elephants here.

Richard *walking side by side with* **Natalie**, *getting further away from* **Sinclair**.

Natalie *(quiet)* What about your new job?

Richard That's fine . . . they're very serious.

Natalie *(slow smile)* You mean they don't laugh at your jokes?

Richard And my boss looks rather ill . . . the office is amazing, it's all decaying, but they're quite efficient . . . it's OK. *(He looks her full in the face.)* Are you happy?

Natalie Oh yes.

Richard But this isn't you, is it? . . . This house . . . and everything?

Natalie Oh, it's me all right. *(She turns on the path, looking lovely.)* It's very much me.

Richard *(watching her)* Really? Even though you never get to speak . . . *(Quiet.)* You do remember don't you . . . *(Touching necklace.)*

Natalie *(quiet smile)* You keep saying that – I don't know what you mean.

Sinclair *behind them on the path.*

Sinclair Do I pass?

Richard (*looking back down the path*) What?

Sinclair (*calling out, waving his hat*) Do I pass? Do I meet with the brother's approval?

Richard (*smiles*) Oh yes.

Natalie Very definitely.

Interior: 'Urban Alert' offices: Day:

Wide shot of the office, and then we move closer to **Richard** *and* **Jessica**. **Richard** *in full flood, talking to* **Jessica** *through the partition.*

Richard It was really rather astonishing, the house and . . . and, it's like being *inside* a colour supplement, pretty women draped about the place, golden-haired children, food on every available surface.

Jessica *watching him closely.*

Jessica Were you envious?

Richard Envious, no, no. (*He smiles.*) Maybe a little. It would drive me mad in less than a week living like that.

Jessica Are you close you two, you and your sister?

Richard Not particularly no. (*Definite.*) Not at all. My parents separated when she was a teenager – she went to live with Dad.

Jessica (*smiles*) And now she's married a rich man?

Richard Yes, a complete cop out. (*He grins.*) She applied for a job, he was the boss. She didn't get the job, but she got him! Anyway you must come and see.

Jessica (*amused*) Is that some kind of invitation?

Richard Yeah, maybe.

Jessica Thanks!

Colin's *face suddenly appears round the partition.*

Colin Don't know what you two are up to. Chat, chat, chat. (*Makes derisive movement of his hand.*) Always at it. I want those figures by the end of the day. *Understand.*

He moves off, his face tense and pale.

Richard Jesus – what's the matter with him?

Jessica (*amused smile*) He doesn't like you – that's all. I know you find that impossible to believe.

Richard (*self-mocking smile*) I'm not used to it.

Jessica I know!

Richard *glances around.* **Paula**, *with food boxes, is waving at him from across the office, a playful wave.* **Jessica** *watching things, amused.*

Interior: 'Urban Alert' offices: Day:

Cut to plans on large graph paper, beautifully drawn plans, the pencil moving along the paper. We see **Richard** *bent over the paper, drawing in the afternoon light. He is concentrating very hard. We see the plans in close-up again.*

Suddenly an orange rose drops into shot, drops onto the middle of the plans.

Richard *looks up,* **Natalie** *is standing there, dressed in surprisingly formal clothes as if for a wedding reception, a rich red dress and hat.*

Natalie Hello.

Richard *looks up, the afternoon light is behind her.*

Richard What on earth are you doing here?

Natalie We were just passing on the way to a wedding in Greenwich, couldn't resist dropping by, having a peek. (*She surveys the room.*) Sinclair's here . . . can he come in? He feels a bit over-dressed for this place, because of the wedding.

Sinclair *in grey suit and top hat approaches round the corner, in mid-afternoon light, looking splendid and formidable.*

Sinclair Forgive this invasion Richard. I feel ludicrously incongruous for a place like this.

*He puts the top hat on **Richard**'s desk.*

Richard It's fine . . . don't worry.

Sinclair But Nats was so eager to have a nose around.

Natalie *staring at a pudgy girl in jeans, sandals and baggy sweater, who's working away.*

Natalie So this is what you wanted?

Richard Yes – so it appears.

Sinclair (*looking at the drawings on **Richard**'s desk*) What plans are these? Oh, this is interesting, this is very interesting, Richard. I know about this, as it happens. (*Quiet.*) I feel there may be an obvious solution which nobody seems to have mentioned because they are all so obsessed about the river frontage.

*As **Sinclair** has been saying this, **Richard** and **Natalie**'s eyes meet fleetingly. She has been taking in the place, and picking up some of the things on his desk. Suddenly **Richard** is aware of an odd sensation, the office sounds begin to fade, a phone ringing on the table next to him remains unanswered. **Richard** is watching **Natalie**, he looks down and then up at her again.*

Natalie Shouldn't that phone be answered?

Richard (*turns slowly*) Yes, probably.

The phone stops.

Natalie Sinclair, we've got to go.

Sinclair (*running his finger along the plans, deeply interested*) Yes, just one moment, this is extremely interesting.

Natalie (*leans low by* **Richard**, *whispers*) You don't belong here, this isn't you.

Richard (*smiles*) Oh yes, it is, very definitely.

Natalie (*casually*) I need to see you properly. Talk about something. I'll make an appointment. Can you fit me in?

Richard Sure, why not. Yes.

Natalie Good.

Natalie *moves off,* **Richard** *watches her go, rich light.*

Richard (*picking up the rose*) Do I keep this?

Sinclair (*taking rose*) No. I believe we need that.

Interior: **Richard**'s *flat: Wet afternoon:*

Shot of the television with test match cricket on, a damp field, with the covers on. No cricket.

Richard *pacing in front of the television. The flat consists of a large room tapering into a much smaller kitchen and bedroom, but it is a fine atmospheric room. Outside there is some large building works, the sound of scaffolding falling, being thrown about, through the whole scene.*

The doorbell rings, **Natalie** *is standing there.*

Richard You're four hours late.

Natalie I'm sorry – I had to go shopping for Sinclair. (*Putting the bags down.*)

Richard Is this deliberate? I've been stuck in here waiting. I couldn't go out!

Natalie *You* were late for lunch! Even later than this!

Richard So it *is* deliberate!

Natalie What's the matter with you Richard!

Richard At least I might have been able to watch the cricket – but it's raining for fuck's sake! It hasn't even started!

Natalie Sssh relax – for Chrissake. (*Involuntarily touching him.*)

Richard You're wearing that again – (*Touches necklace.*)is that on purpose too?

Natalie Maybe this time, yes.

Their eyes meet for a second. Pause. **Richard** *surprised by this admission.*

Natalie Anyway this is not much of a greeting, you haven't even shaved.

Natalie *touches his cheek, and then finds she's kissing him, a full kiss on the lips, but quite a short kiss. She breaks away, her hand goes up to her lips as if trying to rub it off.*

Natalie I'm sorry – (*Smiles.*)don't know what that was for.

Natalie *moves into the small kitchen.*

So this was what was for lunch was it?

Some carrots are boiling in a saucepan on the stove. Nothing else.

Richard *moves after her into the kitchen. Suddenly they are kissing again, she is pressed up against the wall of the tiny kitchen, next to the stove. This time they are much more passionate and sexual as they kiss.* **Natalie** *breaks away.*

Natalie Come on, this is . . . this is . . . (*She moves.*) OK, it just happened. We won't mention it again.

Richard Yes, I knew you'd say that.

Natalie (*switching off the gas on stove*) I don't know why it happened – but it's stopped. It's over . . . let me look at your flat.

She opens the bedroom door. Immediately shuts it. Nervous laugh.

Natalie Don't want to go in there. How many girls have been in there recently?

Richard (*watching her*) Hardly any, I've been very celibate.

Natalie Really? (*Moving into the large room.*) This is nice.

Richard I spent my savings on this place.

Richard *touches her from the back, kisses the nape of her neck.*

Natalie No . . . this is not a good idea.

But she lets him kiss the back of her neck.

Natalie Please Richard . . . I shouldn't have started this . . . we don't mention it. Go. And sit over there.

Richard Is that an order?

They sit opposite each other, on either side of the room.

Natalie (*flicking her hair back*) So is it convenient?

Richard (*nervous grin*) Convenient?

Natalie This flat, for buses?

Richard For buses? (*He flicks off his shoes,* **Natalie** *looks away.*)

Natalie Yes, buses. (*She does the button up on her blouse.*)

Richard (*taking a ginger biscuit out of an old packet*) I think there are probably some buses.

Natalie (*moving her hair again*) What number? The buses?

Richard (*munching soggy biscuit*) I don't know . . . you know

small buses, those small buses that beetle about . . .
Hoppers.

Natalie (*staring at him*) Hoppers . . . you've got some
crumbs . . .

Richard's *hand goes up to his mouth.*

Natalie (*undoes the button on her blouse*) The cricket has
started.

*Highlights of a dramatic one-day game played in a thunderstorm
being shown on the television silently.*

Richard No, that's old highlights.

Natalie (*staring at the white figures in the thunderstorm on TV*) I
never knew they ever played cricket when it rains.

*Pause. Their eyes meet. They move at the same moment, the same
impulse towards each other, kissing passionately, pulling each
other's shirt and blouse off.*

*We cut to close-up of the cricket in the rain. English and Australian
cricketers, dramatic light, dense rain, but also the sun is out, the
water dripping off the players.*

We cut back to **Natalie** *lying on top of* **Richard** *on the floor.
Both of them are naked.*

Natalie (*quiet*) You're going to stop me aren't you? (*She's
kissing him.*) You're going to stop me.

Richard I don't know.

Natalie Come on stop me. (*She half kisses him, stops.*) I'm
just lying here, I'm not doing anything.

Richard (*warm smile*) OK . . .

Natalie OK what? (*Pause.*) Are you clean, are you clean
everywhere?

Richard (*nervous laugh*) Yes of course.

Natalie I don't believe it, maybe you are . . . (*She can't stop* *herself kissing him.*) Stop me . . . (*She smiles.*) Please . . . (*She can't stop the kisses.*) Please . . . (*She continues to kiss.*) Please . . . stop me.

Richard *breaks away, gets up.*

Natalie (*quiet*) I knew you would.

Richard (*nervous grin*) I'm just putting some music on . . . I . . .

He looks for tape, they're scattered everywhere, he just bangs on the radio.

Natalie *comes up beside him, they kiss against the wall.*

Natalie Oh Richard.

We cut to the cricket, the rain and the players, water dripping everywhere, and then back to **Richard** *and* **Natalie** *not trying to resist any more, kissing longingly. Entwined together, kissing passionately.*

Interior: **Richard**'s *flat: Rain heavier:*

They're lying in a corner of the room, curled together, naked and quiet.

Natalie That noise.

Richard It's the scaffolding.

Sound of it dropping.

Natalie Must drive you mad.

Richard No, I like it . . . I don't know why. (*She kisses him, a sexual kiss.*) And to think we never really liked each other as kids. (*Another kiss.* **Natalie** *stops decisively.*)

Natalie OK, that's the last bit.

Richard What do you mean, 'last bit'?

Natalie It just happened.

Richard (*smiles*) 'And we don't mention it. Don't know what got into us' etc, etc.

Natalie (*lightly*) Precisely . . . it's never going to happen again. It's your fault for being away so long.

Richard (*lightly*) It's always my fault.

Natalie Of course.

Natalie *puts his shirt on, and walks over to the kitchen.*

Natalie I'm going to make the carrots – with lots of butter.

Richard They'll be the best I've ever tasted I'm sure.

Natalie (*by stove, half to herself*) We tried to stop it happening and it's finished. (*She glances up from stove.*) By the way Sinclair wants to have lunch with you.

Richard Sinclair. Jesus! You mention that now.

Natalie (*stirring carrots calmly*) Sure . . . (*She looks up.*) There's no problem is there?

Interior: Atrium of office block: Day:

Cut to atrium of a huge new office building with the customary glass lifts gliding up and down its sides. **Richard** *staring about him,* **Sinclair** *appears suddenly from the right of frame.*

Sinclair Here you are! Good! Just have to drop something off – come with me.

Cut to them going up together in a glass lift.

Sinclair These lifts are interesting.

Richard *staring down at the people miles below, as the lift gets higher and higher.*

Richard Are they?

Sinclair Yes – they've become such a common feature, but people hate them, they much prefer the old claustrophobia, now they all have to pretend they don't suffer from vertigo – and feel so *exposed*. (*He gesticulates.*) Everybody can see them! Imagine coming out of a truly terrible meeting and seeing right down there.

Richard *reluctant to look down.*

Sinclair It's frightening! But nobody admits it.

Cut to them moving down large passage with huge doors.

Sinclair These doors are interesting aren't they – ridiculously large. People try to proclaim their importance in such a crass fashion. What will a historian make of these doors?

Richard (*amused smile*) You're interested in everything Sinclair.

Sinclair Oh yes, lifts, doors . . . (*He looks at* **Richard**.) this secretary here, *you* . . . Just stay there for a moment. (*To the Secretary.*) He's expecting me.

Sinclair *goes through one of the massive doors, the Secretary eyes* **Richard** *coldly.*

Sudden euphoric laughter from behind the door, **Sinclair** *sharing a joke, the laughter climbs louder and louder.*

Sinclair *emerging through large door, he smiles.*

Sinclair All done. Simple.

Interior: Bar: High up, view over London: Day:

Cut to **Sinclair** *and* **Richard** *having a drink,* **Sinclair** *incisive, leaning towards* **Richard**.

Sinclair You see I believe in a personal service. People are amazed and flattered that I deliver files of data myself, *walk* around with them! I'm successful enough now for it not to seem a sign of weakness. So many people pretend they're busy don't they, meetings about meetings, most of it is bullshit – just a way of protecting themselves. I like to get to know people.

Richard (*sips drink*) Of course.

Sinclair I like to find out about my clients, poke into their personal lives, and I can tell you there's some interesting things going on, so much *cocaine* being taken – drink too, that's massively on the increase, sudden hysterical temper tantrums flaring up from nowhere –

Richard (*mischievous smile, looking straight at him*) Do *you* have a temper Sinclair?

Sinclair Oh yes, horrendous, unfortunately . . . (*He leans forward.*) We're having one of our great picnics soon. They are not to be missed. You must be there. (*He drinks, puzzled tone.*) Natalie didn't want you to come for some reason.

Close-up at **Richard**.

Interior: 'Urban Alert' offices: Day:

We move with **Richard** *as he enters the office in the early morning light.* **Jessica***'s face tense and pale, the small pudgy girl blowing her nose like a trumpet, the atmosphere awkward and hushed.*

Richard (*at his desk*) So what's the matter? What's happened . . . What's going on?

Jessica It's about Colin. He's sent us a memo. Yours should be somewhere. (*Staring at his mass of papers.*) He's ill.

Richard Yes. I thought so . . . I knew he might be. (*Pause.*

He reads the memo. He looks up surprised. His eyes flick across towards **Colin**.)

Jessica Don't stare – don't do that.

Richard I'm sorry. I didn't know he was gay.

Jessica He isn't.

Richard (*quiet*) He's not?

Jessica He's had it for some time. *I* knew, actually. He's letting the office know because he may be spending more time in hospital. (*Watching* **Richard**.) Don't worry.

Richard (*sharp*) I wasn't.

Jessica You don't need to talk to him about it. Life goes on as normal.

Richard (*quiet*) Yes, of course.

Jessica So get to work.

Exterior: Lift of Docklands Light Railway: Evening:

Richard *running for the lift just as its heavy doors are closing.*

Richard Hold it!

He gets to the lift, the doors close.

Richard Thanks.

He sees he's alone with **Colin** *as the heavy lift grinds upwards.* **Colin** *glances at him perfectly normally, his usual sharp expression.* **Richard** *embarrassed for a moment, not certain whether to say anything.*

Richard Hi.

Colin I want to see the Threepenny Street plans by the end of the week, OK?

Richard Yes of course. I'll make sure that happens.

The lift clanks downwards.

Exterior: Canary Wharf: Day:

Cut to **Colin** *and* **Richard** *walking along by the river. The great development behind them. It is very windy.*

Colin (*moving off*) So don't forget – I've got a very full diary, so the sooner the better.

Richard Understood.

Colin *moving down pavement.*

Richard Have a nice . . .

Colin *turns.*

Have a good weekend.

Exterior: The picnic: A field near the river: Day:

A crane shot, the picnic spread below us. The Bentley parked in the middle of a field of long grass and poppies, hampers bursting with food spread around. Girls in orange dresses, the atmosphere is drenched in sensuality.

Natalie *has a red umbrella/parasol shielding her from the sun.* **Richard** *is taking photographs.* **Jessica** *is lying there, drinking in the sun.* **Sinclair** *pouring himself wine,* **Philippa** *is rubbing cream on herself. The children are picking flowers and looking for snakes.*

Philippa (*rubbing herself with cream*) The sun is getting hotter every year. I heard in New Zealand –

Sinclair (*knowingly*) New Zealand. Ah!

Richard *photographing* **Natalie**, *she keeps moving her head.*

Philippa People were getting burnt, when they've never been burnt before.

Sinclair Wouldn't it be interesting, if because of the greenhouse effect, people started using parasols again. So we ended this century using them just as they did at the end of the last. Maybe you could market them Richard, make your fortune.

Natalie (*with red parasol*) They do look good.

The shadow on her face, **Richard** *close to her with the camera.*

Sinclair Of course there will be winds of 170 miles an hour too, storms like we've never seen, umbrellas will not be much help during those!

Richard *continues to take pictures of* **Natalie**, *their eyes meet,* **Natalie** *telling him silently to stop.* **Sinclair** *is still talking in the background.*

Sinclair And these miniature hurricanes we've been having are going to get worse and worse, trees in southern England are going to become something of a rarity.

Jessica So you're a disaster freak are you?

Sinclair No, these are just facts.

As **Richard** *moves closer to* **Natalie**, *lazy movements over the picnic food,* **Philippa** *is watching* **Natalie** *under her parasol.*

Philippa (*to* **Jessica**) Did you know her *before*?

Jessica Before?

Philippa Before Sinclair of course. (*Whispering as she gazes at* **Natalie**.) He's changed her completely apparently – I wonder if she's really clever enough for him.

Close-up of **Natalie**, *we can't tell if she's heard or not.*

Natalie (*getting up, stretching her body*) I need to go for a walk.

We cut to them crossing a field of blue herbs with **Philippa** *carrying the parasol, and the children running behind.*

We then cut to them moving along a narrow path running along the river bank, the water glimpsed to the left, through the leaves. Couples are entwined in the grass, enjoying the sun, half hidden by the leaves.

Natalie *is moving ahead along the path, occasionally looking back towards* **Richard***, on the path.* **Richard** *follows her.*

Sinclair Look for mushrooms, Nats – but don't kill us, you know the ones to pick.

Natalie *stoops to pick a mushroom,* **Richard** *gets up to her.*

Natalie You shouldn't be here.

Richard Don't be silly.

Natalie *moves off.*

Richard (*half whispered*) Natalie!

Richard *moves fast after her, he stops her on a little boating jetty, where the path opens out.*

We cut between them on the jetty and the rest of the group catching them up, looking towards them.

Richard I need to see you.

Natalie Listen we agreed.

Richard We agreed nothing – and you want to see me . . . we just can't pretend it never happened.

Natalie (*staring at him*) Can't we?

Richard Don't you want to talk about it, ask why?

Natalie No.

Richard Is it because . . . our parents are dead, is it because we didn't see each other for a long time, or . . .

Natalie There *isn't* a reason.

Richard That's right.

Richard *can't take his eyes off her, her brown arms, her summer clothes, she looks so self-possessed.*

Natalie Please don't touch me.

Richard *touches her.*

Natalie Sinclair's coming – he can see.

Richard He'll just think –

Natalie I don't want him to think anything.

Richard You are just my sister, what can he think?

Cut to **Sinclair** *and* **Jessica** *moving along towpath.*

Jessica (*staring at them on the jetty*) What do you think they are talking about?

Sinclair (*smiles, unabashed*) Me, I shouldn't wonder.

Richard (*close to* **Natalie***, more forceful*) Please . . .

Close-up of **Natalie.**

Interior: Conservatory: Evening:

Sinclair*'s head tilted back, his hat down over his eyes,* **Jessica** *picking at some grapes,* **Richard** *is sitting opposite her, but he is watching* **Natalie** *who is in the hall, taking her shoes off.*

Richard *moves into the hall.*

Intercut with:

Interior: Hall: Evening:

Richard (*whispers*) So where?

Natalie Where what?

Richard Where can we meet?

Natalie You're not going to take no for an answer. (*Decisive.*) Maybe we need a proper meeting to clear this up.

Richard (*whispers*) Exactly.

Shot of **Sinclair***, sitting dreamily in chair.*

Natalie I'm not coming to you again. It's just possible – occasionally I go out of town for work.

Richard (*teasing, dismissive*) Oh yes, the employment agency.

Natalie Thank you! Nearly made me change my mind . . . sometimes I go away to interview people. Perhaps I can say I'm doing that.

Richard (*very close to her*) Yes.

Natalie Don't whisper like that – I don't want us to look as if we are plotting.

Richard But we are!

Natalie (*whispering*) But I'm just making normal arrangements with my brother.

Sinclair (*suddenly calling, from conservatory*) Tell her she doesn't need to do that job. Pokey little agency, it's ridiculous.

Natalie (*lightly*) I'm a partner in it now.

Sinclair Oh, makes all the difference! Tell her it's silly just to work for work's sake, meeting morons every day. (*Pulling hat down.*) She won't listen to me.

Natalie (*stops whispering but pulls* **Richard** *close*) We can meet in Sinclair's parents' flat.

Richard (*truly astonished*) What! Are you crazy! What are you trying to do?

Sinclair *looks up idly from conservatory, then tilts back his head again.*

Natalie (*calm*) Don't worry, they're away on a cruise. I've got the keys, I often use it when I'm in town. It's being redecorated, it's a bit grotty . . . but it's somewhere to talk. (*She stares at him.*) But this won't be for a fortnight Richard, if at all.

Richard I can't wait that long.

Natalie (*softly*) Oh yes, you can. Yes you can . . .

Interior: **Natalie** *and* **Sinclair**'s *bedroom: Night:*

Natalie *in white nightdress,* **Sinclair** *lying naked, half covered by sheet. It is extremely hot, they are both sweating. She rolls over, as we cut into the scene, as if they've just finished sex. She looks quite happy. She kisses* **Sinclair**'s *shoulder.*

Natalie I do love you.

Sinclair (*self-mocking smile*) Of course you do.

Natalie Do you love me?

Sinclair Of course I do.

Natalie Even though . . . I'm just me?

Sinclair What does that mean?

Natalie I don't know – (*Pause. Slight smile.*) IT'S ONLY ME – (*Pause.*) go on, you can read it, I don't mind. (*She smiles.*) I can see you edging towards it.

Sinclair *picks up a volume of Proust in French.*

Sinclair Just one chapter. (*Warm smile.*) It's the only thing that shuts me up, isn't it? (*He starts reading. Pause.*)

Natalie (*watching him*) I may have to go away, one weekend . . . I don't know, it's not decided.

Sinclair No problem.

Natalie (*staring at him*) It may be cancelled . . .

Interior: **Natalie**'s *office: Day:*

Cut to a medium-sized high street office in a nondescript Surrey town. Hot warm light. **Natalie** *is sitting at her desk conducting an interview with a small balding man.*

Balding Man Yes, before that I worked for Tesco's, deputy store manager, quite a big branch, just off the M25, and then before that in Guildford. I was acting deputy manager at –

Natalie *is not making notes, a drop of sweat falls on the form. She is curling one of the ends of her hair. The* **Balding Man** *stops, watches her. She looks up, their eyes meet. He senses she's in some sort of sexual reverie.*

Natalie Just a moment . . . (*She grabs any piece of paper off her desk.*) I need to get copies of this.

She moves off, she's kicked off her shoes under desk.

We cut to **Natalie** *by the photostat machine in back room. Without putting any paper in, she switches on the machine. She leans against the wall, puts one of her bare legs up on the wall opposite. The photostat machine flashing green. The room is in shadow. A woman appears in the doorway of the room.*

Natalie Ah, Doreen – I . . . I . . . will be away next weekend. If my husband should ring and mention it – you *will* remember that.

Their eyes meet.

Natalie It's just . . . I *have* to do something, Doreen.

Interior: Mansion flats: Lobby: Afternoon:

Key shots of **Natalie** *standing in a fine dress, coat over her arm, calm, poised, one suitcase by her side, in the lobby of grand old mansion flats, evocative light.* **Richard** *comes towards her – the shot pulling him, drawing him closer.*

Richard I am on time, aren't I?

Natalie (*slight smile*) Yes, for once, you are.

They begin to move up the staircase. An old upper-middle class woman, an inhabitant of the flats, is coming down with a shopping trolley, **Richard** *helps her down the last few steps, watching* **Natalie** *as he does so. Old woman mutters, glancing at their faces beadily.*

Interior: Mansion flat: Afternoon:

Richard *and* **Natalie** *come in to mansion flat – which has extremely large rooms, fine plaster ceilings, huge windows with lace curtains, blowing gently in the breeze, a balcony and balustrade overlooking a sleepy leafy garden square, a richly evocative square. The furniture is heavy and old, the colours subdued greys, greens, browns,* **Natalie** *in her bright dress moving amongst them.*

Richard Jesus, it's like Rosemary's Baby! This place. It's enormous.

They move about the flat, avoiding each other, skirting past each other, not touching as they explore. **Richard** *takes off his jacket as he moves,* **Natalie** *puts down her coat, lets down her hair. Moments later she has kicked off her shoes.*

Natalie (*as she does this*) Sinclair's grandfather made a fortune out of margarine, before the First World War . . . they had three flats like this once.

Richard (*staring out at the leafy old gardens*) Margarine . . . so long ago, I didn't know the money went back that far . . . I love these sleepy old gardens.

Natalie (*moving, businesslike*) We're just going to talk, OK, that's all . . . get things . . . get things . . .

Richard *touches her as he moves past her, turns her around.*

Natalie (*a slight excited laugh*) Out in the open.

They start to kiss, unable to stop touching each other, passionately entwined, **Richard** *unbuttoning her dress, pulling it off above her head, in the mouth of the cupboard, among all the old elderly clothes and shoes. They fall down together at the base of the cupboard and begin to make love.*

Interior: Mansion flat: Early evening:

Cut to **Richard** *and* **Natalie** *lying on their fronts, naked on the bed, as if after sex. But apart, not touching. The linen on the bed, starched, crisp.*

Richard It's so warm. (*Stretching his arm out.*) It's great. Why do you think . . .

Natalie (*calmly*) No whys.

Richard (*smiles*) You don't know what I was going to say.

Sound of a key in lock, front door opens, **Richard** *sits up looking startled. Very alarmed. Small mid-European cleaning woman bustles into hall, they can see her through the open bedroom door. She is hunting for something, nosing around.*

Natalie It's all right – Just get under the sheets. Come on. And *sleep*!

Natalie *calmly gets up, pulling on stylish dressing gown out of her half unpacked suitcase. She intercepts cleaner.*

Natalie Hello Selina, you've forgotten your keys have you? Yes?

Cleaning woman snuffling around, looks straight into bedroom.

Natalie My brother's sleeping in here. See – sleeping, like a baby. I'm getting ready for the theatre, giving myself a treat. (*She smiles.*) I'm up in town on business.

Cleaning woman muttering in some incomprehensible language, disappears, bangs front door.

Natalie *turns, laughing.*

Natalie Don't look so worried!

Interior: Mansion flat: Night:

Night. **Richard** *and* **Natalie** *in loose summer clothes sitting in semi-darkness on the floor of the biggest room, passing a wine bottle between them. Fruit from a jug, mangoes, apricots, oranges. During the scene* **Natalie** *rolls them over to* **Richard**. *Very little light.*

Natalie (*laughing*) Sometimes . . . I feel this big with Sinclair. (*Fingers close together.*) No, this big . . . (*Getting smaller.*) Even this big.

Richard *is smiling at her.*

Natalie It's nice being able to tell someone . . . at last. (*Wipes a dribble of wine from the corner of his mouth, fondly.*) That's all that's going on here, *understand*?

Richard Of course. (*Pause.*) *What* happens if he tries to ring you?

Natalie He won't. Not tonight. Fortunately he's out. Tomorrow I have to remember.

Richard Oh, really? Out? What's he doing? What's he up to? Maybe he's cheating too.

Natalie (*emphatic*) This isn't cheating. Absolutely not. Anyway, that's an American expression.

Richard (*solemn*) Is he faithful?

Natalie (*slowly saying the word*) Faithful. Yes, I think so. (*Slight laugh.*) It's never really occured to me he wasn't. (*Staring at* **Richard**.) We can see – he always works on a Saturday morning. Even when we have people over for lunch, he insists on going in. Nothing stops him. (*Looking into* **Richard***'s eyes*.) We can take a look at him tomorrow.

Interior: City office building: Foyer: Day:

Subjective shot of the modern foyer, **Natalie** *beginning to move across foyer,* **Richard** *behind her.*

Richard But don't they know you, here?

Natalie I don't think so, no. I hardly ever come . . . we'll see.

Natalie *up to reception desk,* **Stoney-Faced Woman**.

Natalie I wonder . . . if you could see if Sinclair Bryant is in his office.

Stoney-Faced Woman Mr Bryant? One moment.

She phones up, shot of **Richard** *watching.*

Richard (*whispers*) What you going to say if he *is* there . . . this is silly.

Natalie *seemingly totally calm, gives the woman a little smile, stares straight at her.*

Stoney-Faced Woman No reply.

Natalie What?

Stoney-Faced Woman (*as if for a two-year-old child*) There is – no – reply.

Natalie *looks startled.*

Exterior: Road outside City office: Day:

Natalie *walking along slightly in front of* **Richard**.

Natalie I don't know . . . I don't know what I feel. He's probably just . . .

Wide shot of **Natalie** *from across the street. We see her suddenly stop dead in her tracks.* **Richard** *who hadn't noticed, has to go back to fetch her.* **Natalie** *is staring through glass window of a cafe.*

Richard What's the matter?

He looks down at one of the tables. In front of them is **Sinclair** *eating a quite enormous breakfast – a fry-up spilling over three plates, with fried bread, mushrooms, sausage, eggs, tomatoes, chips, even a piece of steak.* **Sinclair** *is eating voraciously and reading.*

Natalie *presses herself against the glass, fascinated, amused.* **Richard** *pulls her away, but she moves back for a second look.*

Richard (*suddenly loud*) Natalie – come here!

Natalie *turns her head, across the street her car is being clamped, it is parked almost opposite the restaurant on the other side of the road.*

Natalie Jesus! That's all we need!

She runs across the road, and up to the men doing the clamping. **Richard** *follows.*

Natalie (*although excited, she is not hysterical, in command*) Now that is not fair – absolutely not. We've only been here ten seconds, twenty seconds at the most.

Clamping Officer I'm afraid, once the clamps are out of the van madam – there is no going back.

Richard (*eyeing the restaurant across the road*) Natalie, please, you're meant to be in Nuneaton. Come away, come on, you can never ever talk your way out of a clamp.

Close-up of **Natalie** *staring into the eyes of the* **Clamping Officer**.

Natalie (*very direct*) I'm having an affair with that man there.

Indicating **Richard** *who is peering at the other clamps in the van, trying to distance himself.*

Natalie And my husband is right across the street having breakfast, and about to come out. (*Slight smile, gazing at* **Officer**.) You wouldn't want to break up my life would you?

Officer's *face intrigued. Shot of clamping van roaring off, and* **Richard** *and* **Natalie** *jumping into car, double quick.*

Richard What on earth did you say to him?

Natalie (*laughing*) Let's celebrate.

Interior: Jewellery shop: Day:

Natalie *with several carrier bags from expensive shops, peering at jewellery with* **Richard**. *A very sober male shop assistant watches them.*

Natalie I want to get something for Sinclair . . . (*To* **Shop Assistant**.) I want something for my husband.

Shop Assistant (*to* **Richard**) What do you like the look of sir?

Natalie (*smiles*) No point asking him! I think that gold tie pin looks nice.

(Photo: Simon Mein)

(Photo: Simon Mein)

Natalie phones Sinclair to lie about her whereabouts.
'I'd hate to have a real affair.'

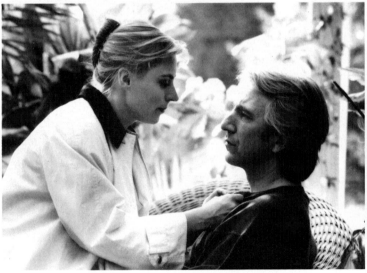

(Photo: Simon Mein)

Natalie returns to Sinclair after her illicit weekend.

Richard and Natalie make love in the empty apartment.

(Photo: Simon Mein)

Richard, unable to extract himself from the affair, waits for Natalie in the hotel.

The fight on the road on the day of the party.

(Photo: Simon Mein)

Sinclair, Richard and Natalie walk among the bonfires
at the end of the summer.

Richard Does he use tie pins? (*Correcting himself.*) Do *I* use tie pins?

A giggly exuberant mood between them.

Natalie Oh yes. They're very fashionable again. We'll take it.

Interior: Mansion flat: Night:

Evening light, dying in the big room. **Natalie** *comes out of the bedroom in a beautiful new evening dress.* **Richard** *stares across the room at her, rather overwhelmed at the sight of her. Deep sense of attraction and love from him.*

Natalie (*makes a self-mocking fanfare noise*) Do you like it?

Close-up of **Richard**.

Cut to **Natalie** *with phone, dialling the last number.* **Richard** *near her.*

Natalie This is important, don't distract me. (*Phone is answered.*) Sinclair?

Interior: The kitchen: Evening:

Sinclair *on phone in kitchen. We intercut with* **Natalie**.
Sinclair *during conversation is trying to extract a knife from the washing-up machine which is open and bulging with dirty plates and cutlery. At the beginning of sequence he opens a drawer to find no clean knives left.*

Sinclair Natalie . . . great. I was just wondering when you'd ring.

Intercut with:

Interior: Mansion flat: Evening:

Natalie I'm fine. Bit tired . . . fine.

Richard *touching her hand during the conversation, kisses her neck, running his hand down her neck, over her arms, over her breasts.* **Natalie***'s head goes back.*

Sinclair How's the hotel?

Natalie A little gloomy . . . but the rooms are very big . . . (*Trying to push* **Richard** *away but responding to him.*)

Sinclair Yes . . . those big old provincial hotels can be very depressing, how's the food?

Natalie The food. (*She smiles.*) You would ask that! The food . . .

Richard *kissing her.*

Natalie Excellent, I'm just going out to get a quick bite now . . . and then I'm going straight to bed. Very early tonight, OK?

Sinclair OK my darling.

Natalie *about to ring off.*

Sinclair How are the beds?

Natalie The beds? The beds are . . . I've only got a single – average, I'd say. Quite nice.

Sinclair Fine. Good. Is there a view?

Natalie (*her head goes back*) No. No view – not to speak of, not here in Nuneaton. Goodnight, darling. (*She rings off, kissing* **Richard***, just brushing his lips, not real kisses.*) I'd hate to have a real affair. Lies . . . deceit . . . all that.

Exterior: Canary Wharf by the river: Night:

Richard *and* **Natalie** *walking in the hot summer night, her dress shining.*

Richard You don't feel –

Natalie No questions, I told you they were forbidden.

Richard (*lightly*) You're so calm, we're doing something illegal, a major taboo, could go to gaol! – and you just seem to find it mildly relaxing!

Natalie We're not doing anybody any harm; we're not sticking needles into our arms, killing ourselves with drink. Just enjoy it, the last moments.

Richard What if it wasn't the last moments?

Natalie What do you mean?

They move around a corner, searchlights are stabbing the sky as if for an opening of a nightclub by the river, among the otherwise dead offices.

Richard I mean we could go off together somewhere.

Natalie Like where?

Richard (*lightly*) I don't know. Mexico. People always go to Mexico in stories and things, don't they, when they are fugitives.

Natalie But we're not fugitives. And how would we live?

Richard (*charming smile*) Oh there are plenty of ways of making money. We could write a blockbuster novel, you know the sort you buy in airports, that's easy enough, or – (*He suddenly turns.*) I *mean it. We can both escape!*

Natalie *looks alarmed at this.*

Natalie (*touching him*) Sssh . . . stop it . . . we can't go anywhere, don't think it, not even as a joke.

They get to where the searchlights are positioned, revolving round. Kids standing outside the club, some in very short skirts.

Richard (*looks at the kids*) Being single –

Natalie What about it?

Richard It's not as simple as it used to be.

Natalie (*touching him*) Suddenly feeling older are you? – my little brother . . .

Interior: The kitchen: Night:

Cut to pouring water, gushing from the washing-up machine. It has already half flooded the kitchen. **Sinclair** *rushes into the kitchen.*

Sinclair Shit! . . . Christ!

Rips out plug from washing-up machine, water still spilling from pipe somewhere behind the machine, leaking.

Sinclair Calm . . . calm . . . come on, be calm. (*Pulls out 'Yellow Pages'.*) No, no, wait a minute, no rip-offs. (*His hand flicking through 'useful numbers' by phone.*) Nats will know . . . (*He dials briskly.*)

Shot of the water dribbling from behind the machine.

Sinclair Is that the Royal George? – I want to speak to Mrs Natalie Bryant . . . what . . . ? sorry . . . what? What do you mean there's nobody of that name? Don't be ridiculous. (*Slowly.*) Mrs Natalie Bryant – you *are* in Nuneaton are you? Then check again. I may have got the name of the hotel wrong, but it's highly unlikely . . . Right! Give me the number of *every* hotel in Nuneaton. It's urgent, there's a flood in the kitchen.

Close-up of **Sinclair**'*s face, puzzled, truly startled.*

Interior: All-night supermarket: Night:

A shot of **Sinclair** *pushing large wire basket through supermarket, deep in thought, muttering slightly.*

Sinclair Let's get this straight . . . the hotels . . . all the hotels . . . stop talking to yourself.

He sits on the floor for a moment to do his shoe-lace up, not an abject figure, but a deeply thoughtful one, coping with a possibility he'd never considered.

Sinclair There is an explanation . . . must be.

Cut to **Sinclair** *at the check-out, still with his large wire basket, the only thing in it is one packet of kitchen roll. He stares down at it.*

Sinclair (*to check-out girl*) This looks silly doesn't it? I was actually looking for something more substantial, a . . . a . . . looking for some absorbant . . .

Check-out girl looks bewildered.

Sinclair Something to *absorb* . . . a towel would do really, of course but, maybe I'll get another packet of this, do you think?

Interior: Bedroom: Night:

Sinclair *going through* **Natalie**'s *drawers.*

Sinclair (*muttering*) No, this is too much, don't do this . . .

He stops himself, takes one more final riffle through her things, then stops himself again.

Sinclair Stop it . . . Stop *it.* (*He sits on the end of the bed.*) Do things logically.

Interior: Mansion flats: Bedroom: Morning:

Early morning sun, through the net curtains. **Natalie** *and*
Richard*'s faces close to each other,* **Richard** *staring at*
Natalie*'s sleeping face. He gets out of bed, naked, moves towards
the curtains. Church bells are ringing from the square, Sunday
morning bells. He looks out at the golden peaceful square.* **Natalie**
opens her eyes.

Richard (*gesturing at the view*) You know this place can
have hardly changed in the last fifty years . . . it's a time
warp, isn't it.

Natalie (*quiet*) Yes.

Richard Be nice to stay here, wouldn't it?

Natalie (*quiet, staring from bed*) *No.*

Exterior: Church and square: Sunday morning:

Richard *and* **Natalie** *come out into the sleepy Sunday morning
square. He is wearing a shirt and jeans and is barefoot,* **Natalie** *a
short skirt and T-shirt. The bells are ringing out.*

Richard We don't *need* to go back yet. Don't you see . . .
(*Lightly.*) we really don't . . .

Natalie (*suddenly up to him, pushing him against a brick wall in
the sun*) Now listen to me . . . we don't see each other –
listen! . . . we don't even set eyes on each other, until
you're going out with someone. Got yourself a girlfriend.

Richard You're setting me tasks now!

Natalie I'm not seeing you until that happens, because
you're getting addicted to this.

Richard It's only happened twice – that's not addiction.

Natalie (*touching him in the sun, his open shirt*) You see I
fancy you, and I love you as a brother – that's all, and you

fancy me, and you're beginning to love me as a *lover* and that is going to end badly, messily, (*Touching him.*) unless we're careful. Maybe I've always fancied you a little . . . and probably should never have done –

Richard (*cutting her off*) Sssh. (*Pause.*) I find a girlfriend, and then what happens? Can I see you?

Natalie You won't want to then.

Richard But if I do?

Natalie We'll see.

Richard That's a strange bargain. (*He smiles.*) But simple.

Sound of choir practice coming out of the church, before the morning service. **Richard** *smiles.*

Richard Go into the church and feel no guilt. I dare you!

Interior: Church: Day:

They go into the church, a group of young choristers singing, stopping and starting. **Richard** *and* **Natalie** *sit for a moment in a pew listening to the young voices singing.*

Richard (*turns, touches her cheek*) You do look beautiful.

Natalie (*very firm*) I MEAN IT – I PROMISE YOU. (*Her eyes half close.*) Oh Richard, please . . . please, don't try to make this more . . . (*Very fond, touching his hair.*) *I* don't want it to be more.

Interior: Hall/conservatory: Day:

Natalie *arriving back with her shopping bags, moving through the hall to the conservatory,* **Sinclair** *is sitting waiting, very still, with the light behind him.*

Natalie You're in here.

Sinclair (*watching her closely*) So it appears.

Natalie *looking tired, but her eyes still alive, excited.*

Natalie (*with bags*) I went on an orgy of shopping.

Sinclair You had the time?

Natalie I had some of the afternoon off yesterday, between meetings. (*Smile.*) Went on a spree to kill the boredom.

She puts tie pin down in front of him.

Sinclair That's lovely, very useful.

Natalie (*gently*) It's not meant to be useful.

Sinclair I had a disaster with the washing-up machine.

Natalie (*not taking this in, moving in the conservatory*) Doesn't matter. (*Warm.*) You're so hopeless with anything mechanical Sinclair!

Sinclair (*simply*) How was the hotel?

Natalie Gloomy. I told you. (*Lightly.*) Huge and draughty.

Sinclair What was it called? This hotel?

Pause. **Natalie** *with her back to him, she senses something.*

Natalie I told you what it was called.

Sinclair I just wanted to avoid it in the future.

Natalie You've never been to Nuneaton – never likely to go. (*Slight laugh.*) What is this?

Sinclair (*calm*) Fine. I don't need to know . . . I was just curious.

Natalie, *sitting astride him, pinning the tie pin on.*

Natalie The Royal George. (*Fondly.*) And it *is* a good idea to avoid it.

Sinclair (*quiet*) Right. Good.

Natalie *moving her hand down his face.*

Sinclair I'm glad you're back.

Natalie So am I.

Interior: 'Urban Alert' offices: Day:

Mixture of grey evening light, and electric light, all the table lamps on. **Jessica** *sitting behind* **Colin**'s *desk, in his office.* **Richard** *dropping some papers in front of her.*

Jessica Thank you, not before time.

Richard (*lightly, staring at the papers*) I wish we were getting somewhere.

Jessica So do I.

Richard *doesn't move.*

Jessica You haven't been to see Colin in hospital yet, have you?

Richard No, I will, I will . . . I promise. (*Not moving.*)

Jessica You *keep* putting it off. Is there something else?

Richard Jessica – what are you doing tonight? (*He smiles.*) I've been meaning to ask for some time.

Jessica What's that twinkle for?

Richard What twinkle?

Jessica I don't believe this, Richard. The vanity! Just get out of here before I lose my temper.

Richard I was just asking you out.

Jessica I thought you were meant to be something of an – expert. (*Sharp smile.*) You seem decidedly rusty to me.

Richard Rusty? (*He smiles.*) Certainly not. So what's the answer?

Jessica No. *No.* I've never seen somebody so obviously thinking about another . . . (*She stops.*)

Richard Another what?

Jessica (*sharp smile*) I was going to say another woman, but it's more likely to be a fifteen-year-old girl, isn't it? Who is she? At a loose end tonight because of her? Or are you trying to forget her?

Richard (*moving away*) OK. OK, that's OK, Jessica.

Richard *sees through the glass partition, a dark-haired young person in restaurant uniform moving among tables, with take-away boxes.*

Jessica Yes, why don't you try that – much better idea. (*As* **Richard** *moves.*) Why's it so urgent anyway? (*She laughs.*) Can't go one night without!

Richard *goes up to dark-haired person who turns to reveal herself as a stocky fifty-year-old woman.*

Richard (*non-plussed*) Ah. Sorry – I was looking for somebody else. Maybe you know where she is?

Interior/Exterior: Chinese fake world in Trocadero: Night:

Richard *moving from main concourse in Trocadero shopping centre into the fake Chinese 'streets', the narrow passages, the stalls of food, steam, street signs, red and yellow light.* **Paula**, *the first girl he saw with the take-away in the office, is serving out food to a couple of tourists.* **Paula** *sees him, leans out and calls.*

Paula Hi!

Richard So you remember me.

Paula Of course. Come behind here, help me serve some of these tourists. (*Sharp smile.*) Come on, it'll be good for you!

Cut to the false street lights flicking off, **Paula** *and* **Richard** *moving down the 'Chinese street', as the place shuts down, towards the back door and the outside world. Just before they get out,* **Richard** *sees a green neon sign saying 'Gents'.*

Richard Just a moment. (*He smiles.*) I've forgotten something.

Interior: Gents: Night:

Richard *slips into the Gents, where there is a massive Durex machine on the wall, with about ten different varieties, with different refinements. A large Scotsman is studying the choice.*

Scotsman Never know which flavour to pick, do you? (*He looks at* **Richard**.) Which do you get? (*Both stare at machine.*) I always get Strawberry Elite – (*indicating slogan on machine.*) you're 'safer' with Strawberry Elite!

Interior: Chinese fake world: Night:

Richard *emerging out of the lavatory,* **Paula** *watching curious,* **Richard** *with four different packets in his hand, slips them into his pocket.*

Richard (*charming smile*) Sorry to keep you waiting.

They bang through the back door into the alleyway behind.

Exterior: Alleyway behind Trocadero: Evening:

The back street, litter blowing over the pavement. Two girls standing in a seedy entrance, kids in the distance drunkenly marauding the street. Sordid, messy atmosphere.

Paula (*stretches her body, reaching towards the night sky*) Fresh air! At last!

Richard (*picking his way over the garbage*) Fresh air? *This* is fresh air?

Paula Oh yes – when you've had people grabbing at you all day – this is wonderful. (*She moves in front of him.*) Free at last.

Richard *looks around at the sleaze, tramps curled up in a doorway. We feel his disgust. Strong images of young beggars, people wandering in the night or asleep amongst the garbage.*

Paula (*warm smile*) What do you want to do now? Apart from *that* of course.

Richard (*gently*) Not sure I want to do *that*. Not just yet. Can I just be with you a bit. Can I?

Paula Maybe. (*Up to him.*) You know what you're like – you're like somebody who's trying to make an alibi for himself.

Richard Perhaps I am.

Paula An alibi for what?

Richard (*lightly*) Not murder anyway, something infinitely worse than that.

Interior: **Sinclair** *and* **Natalie**'s *bedroom: Night:*

Cut to **Natalie** *and* **Sinclair** *in bed, watching TV. Relaxed intimate atmosphere, sense of them growing together again.*

Sinclair (*pointing at TV*) It's the one with the yellow socks, I keep telling you. It's going to be him.

Natalie (*laughing, playfully hitting him*) Stop it, sssh, you always know what's going to happen! Don't tell me.

Phone rings, beside bed. **Natalie** *answers it.*

Intercut with:

Interior: Phone booth: Street: Night:

Richard It's me.

We intercut with **Richard** *in phone booth, in the back street,* **Paula** *close to the glass.*

Richard We can arrange to meet – your condition's being met . . . fulfilled.

Natalie Richard it is too soon. Much too soon. Who is she?

Shot of **Paula**.

Richard Just somebody I know slightly, why, are you jealous?

Cut to **Natalie**, **Sinclair** *watching TV.*

Natalie Doesn't sound a proper one to me. Can't talk now. (*Whispers.*) I'll think about it. (*She rings off.*) That was Richard – he's got a new girlfriend.

Sinclair Calling you with progress reports at this time of night. He must be drunk!

Natalie (*quiet*) Yes – yes, I think he is.

Interior: **Natalie**'s *dressing room: Night:*

Natalie *slips away into her dressing room, a small private space. She sits at the dressing table, light from an old lamp. She is so hot, sweat running down her neck. She moves a photo of* **Sinclair** *on the dressing table; behind it is a picture of* **Richard** *as we first saw him in the film. Her lips hover close to the picture, her head bends down, as if she is fighting something, torn. She slips the thirties necklace and the photo into a bottom drawer, closes it with a sharp movement. She begins to cry, fighting back tears, silent tears, not sobs.*

Interior: **Paula**'s *room: Very early morning:*

Small, upstairs room, dawn light through little window.

Cut to a cat, its eyes shining straight at us. Then to **Paula***, who is lying sweating in the heat on the bed in T-shirt and panties next to the cat. Outside the window a boy in boxer shorts is roller skating in sleepy jagged circles on a slab of concrete below.* **Paula** *turns her head lazily.* **Richard** *is sitting on a chair, watching her in a detached way. He smiles.*

Paula Haven't you slept?

Richard Don't think so.

Paula It's not right, is it, that it should be as hot as this, in *England*!

Richard *moves over to the bed, begins stroking the cat.*

Richard (*lightly*) Do you worry, Paula?

Paula Worry? What about?

Richard (*gently stroking her leg*) Oh you know, anything and everything . . . the end of the world?

Paula Why bother? (*She smiles.*) Nothing much you can do about that.

Richard (*gently rubbing her bare feet*) And sex?

Paula (*dreamy smile*) What about it? (*Watching him.*) This is nice . . . let's just do this, no more.

Richard (*amused smile*) You mean it's better than nothing?

Paula No, it's too warm to do any more.

Richard (*lightly*) You think about sex a lot, Paula?

Paula You sound like a doctor! Some days I think about nothing else. (*Lightly.*) Around 4 o'clock, usually.

Richard (*tracing a bead of sweat down her leg*) It used to seem so simple, didn't it . . . (*He laughs.*) Except you're probably too young to remember – never had to worry about disease, not something that could kill. But now . . . there is a man at work who has Aids.

Paula Poor guy. I'm sorry.

Richard (*quiet*) Yes.

Paula (*calmly*) I suppose soon almost everybody will know somebody who's got it.

Richard Yes, but him being right there, now, in a strange way it's almost like a sign . . . (*Self-mocking smile.*) from I don't know where – that what I'm doing is right.

Paula (*staring dreamily*) And what are you doing?

Richard (*smiles*) Oh, just trying to escape.

Paula Where is there to go?

Richard Aha!

Paula (*sitting up, her face close to his*) Where are you going? Tell me! What do you have to do?

Richard Oh, I have found a simple way, better than any drug, any desert island.

Paula Really? (*Their eyes meet.*) So what do you need the alibi for?

Richard Oh, nothing very much. I'm just in love with someone.

Paula (*disappointed*) Is that all?

Richard (*smiling*) 'Fraid so.

Paula That's not very dangerous . . . I *knew* you were thinking of someone else.

Interior: Mansion flat: Lobby: Day:

We are inside the lobby waiting with **Richard**. *The porter in shirt sleeves, smoking, wanders out into the hot summer streets. Through the ornamental glass in the doors we see* **Natalie** *approaching dressed in yellow.*

Richard Natalie – I thought you weren't coming.

Natalie I nearly didn't.

Richard (*touching the yellow dress*) Is this new?

Natalie No, not very. (*Immediately breaking away.*) We're not going up; if you've got anything to say to me, you can say it here.

Richard Here?

Natalie Yes – go and sit over there.

Richard (*lightly*) You're always telling me where to sit!

He sits across the foyer, for a moment they are alone, beneath the big mirrors. **Natalie** *has the flat key in her hand, a big, old-fashioned key, she keeps turning it over and over in her fingers.*

Natalie So what do you want?

Richard (*staring across the foyer at her*) I want to touch you.

Natalie I don't want you to.

Richard Let's go up. Just for a little while, come on. (*Watching the key in her lap.*)

Natalie No . . . no . . . I'm not going to let you talk me into it.

Richard I did what you said, your task –

Natalie I don't believe you. I don't believe anything's changed.

Richard *moves his chair a little closer.*

Richard I'm not going to go away, Natalie. It's not something you can suddenly drop. (*He smiles.*)

The old woman we saw before in the flats, starts moving through the door pulling her trolley, making a great business of crossing the foyer, and climbing the stairs, muttering crossly.

Richard (*as the woman appears*) Ignore her . . . (*Lowering his voice.*) Let's go up, Natalie. Just today. It's what we both want. It's what you want.

Close-up of **Natalie**. *We feel she is about to weaken.*

Richard (*charming smile*) Haven't I always been right about you?

Natalie It's not what I want.

Richard (*getting close*) Why did you come then – if you don't want to?

Natalie Sinclair's been asking about the hotel I stayed in.

Richard Really? Did he believe you?

Natalie I think so. I don't know.

Richard Good, then this can last all summer then, can't it? At least . . .

Natalie No, Richard. You see, you really need it, and I won't have that.

The old woman dragging her trolley up in distance, muttering.

Richard (*lightly*) If it's an addiction, like you say, maybe I'm prepared to –

Natalie Don't say that.

Richard Don't say what?

Natalie Say the rubbish you were about to say that you're prepared to 'die' for it because that's crap. You want to pretend this is all going to end tragically, something enormously final, because you find that idea exciting.

Richard (*quiet*) No, that's not true.

Natalie I need you, Richard. I really need you – as a *friend*.

Richard A friend! . . . (*He's up to her, holding her.*) Come on, Natalie, give me the key and –

Natalie Stop that, get off me, go on, GET OFF!

She fights him, raining cuffs on him, the porter outside smoking with his back to them. They see the old woman's face staring at them through the bannisters.

Richard Sssh . . . ssh, Natalie . . . we don't want somebody reporting us.

Natalie (*against the wall*) No . . . (*More lightly.*) we don't want you to go to gaol, do we . . . (*Touches his hair.*) Hadn't you better get back to work?

Richard No, my boss is very ill. I told you he's got Aids.

Natalie Yes, I'm sorry. Have you seen him yet?

Richard No.

Natalie That's very cowardly – why not? You've got to go at once.

Richard You keep setting me tasks!

Natalie Why not? I am your sister, after all.

Richard And if I do go?

Natalie I make no promises. (*Their faces very close.*) You can have one kiss . . . just one. I shouldn't . . . but one kiss can do no harm.

She lets him kiss her, then breaks away.

Natalie If you keep away from me . . . till the end of next month, then you will have proved something to me. You can break it, Richard. I promise you.

She moves back out into the hot London streets. **Richard** *watching her go.*

Exterior: Mansion flat courtyard: Day:

We follow **Natalie** *across the courtyard, see her forcing herself to walk away, wanting to go back.*

Interior: **Sinclair**'s *office: Day:*

Sinclair *in his fine office, tastefully furnished in pale grey and yellow, with modern pictures on the wall. He is sitting behind a striking black desk, totally occupied with a domestic answering machine – listening to calls* **Natalie** *has received, messages that have been left, a mixture of male and female voices. One of his own phones rings on his desk. A secretary is sitting opposite him, waiting patiently.*

Sinclair (*takes the call, while the tape still plays*) Alan? Yes, no. No, I'm fine. I'm busy at the moment. Call you back. OK? (*Watching tape, then looks up at secretary.*) Won't be a moment. This is my home answering machine. (*Matter of* *fact.*) We had a burglary last week. Just seeing if there's anything here, any wrong numbers, anything that doesn't sound right. (*He continues to stare down at tape, listening for a message left by* **Natalie**.)

Interior: Hospital: Day:

Richard *walking through the hospital ward, to the end bed, where* **Colin** *is lying, looking very, very ill, his face swollen with drugs, but his eyes sharply alive.* **Richard** *trying to cover the awkwardness he feels.*

Richard Hello.

Colin Hi. Sit down.

Pause.

Richard I didn't know what to bring – so I brought a couple of books, thrillers –

Colin (*quiet*) Great. Thanks.

Richard There's a third one here – it's got a little messed up, a biro burst in my pocket. (*Produces third book. It's covered in a large stain.*) I've been wondering if I should give it to you . . . (*He smiles.*) but it's the most fun of the three. So there it is . . .

Colin No, give it to me. Fine.

Richard (*looking at book*) I'm sorry, it looks awful. (*He begins instinctively to wipe at it.*)

Colin No problem.

A couple are sitting across the ward, next to a patient finding it very difficult to talk to him.

Colin (*quiet*) You can go when you like – don't feel . . .

Richard Oh, I'm sorry. I didn't mean to look . . .

Colin It's like someone made you come.

Richard *looks guilty.*

Colin (*watching group across ward*) My parents haven't been to see me.

Richard (*startled*) Really? I'm sorry, that's . . .

Colin (*sharp*) That's just like them. True to form.

Pause. **Richard** *fingering inky book, wiping at it.*

Richard I probably should have bought some fruit I know, I'm sorry. It seemed so –

Colin (*very direct*) Stop apologising all the time, it's nauseating – and stop wiping the book like that, it's driving me crazy – I'll read it with the stains. OK! Right!

Richard *grins, the outburst warms up the atmosphere.*

Richard Right. Are you allowed out of bed, out of here, for an afternoon?

Colin Yes, if I want. Can be negotiated.

Richard I've got a meeting with Lappenshaw Mercantile. (*Staring at* **Colin**.) Want to come?

Colin *doesn't react for a moment.*

Richard I could brief you on the way. (*He smiles.*) Why not?

Pause.

Colin Yes. OK. Why not?

Interior: **Natalie**'s *bedroom: Day:*

Cut to **Natalie** *wrapping up jewellery – she puts it into a case, as if beginning to pack up.*

Exterior: Docklands Light Railway: Day:

Cut to **Colin** *and* **Richard** *on the train.* **Colin** *in wheelchair,* **Richard** *sitting next to him in almost empty carriage, studying his papers. The train passing across the extraordinary Docklands urban landscape, rampant, unplanned.*

Richard (*with papers*) I think those are all the important ones. (*Staring at the view.*) Look at it, it's like fighting with a pea-shooter, what we're trying to do.

Colin (*light grin*) Yes, might get one extra zebra crossing – better than nothing.

Richard (*staring out of window*) You know I can remember when they first announced what was going to happen here, it was going to be a great new city, the new Venice, modern but magical – one of the wonders of Europe!

Colin (*laughs*) Yes, I can remember that too.

Richard And look what happened! (*Looks at the chaotic buildings.*)

Colin You're becoming an architectural reactionary, Richard.

Richard No, no, I'm a modernist – definitely. (*He smiles.*) Always *thought* I was.

Colin Oh yeah?

Richard (*suddenly laughing*) This is incredible, isn't it? You're the one that's ill – yet you're the optimist!

Colin Yes. Because you're determined not to be. (*Teasing smile.*) Aren't you? (*Jabbing him, laughing.*) Aren't you?

Richard (*grin*) Maybe.

Colin (*laughs*) We'll have to do something about that, Richard.

Interior: **Natalie**'s *bedroom: Day:*

Cut to **Natalie** *putting a fur coat into a trunk. She is packing winter clothes.*

Interior: Developer's office: Day:

The low black and gold light. **Colin** *wheeled into the office by* **Richard**, *to face* **Geal**, **Noley**, *and third young man.* **Geal** *in the middle of eating sandwiches, looks astonished and deeply uneasy at the sight of* **Colin**. *The wheelchair bearing down on* **Geal**.

Richard Colin was able to make it after all.

Geal (*words almost sticking*) How good to see you. We're a little pressed for time today, so maybe we should –

Colin (*sharp smile*) In that case let's not waste any more of it. (*Flicks his fingers.*) Richard!

Richard *standing behind him handing him papers on command.*

Colin Right, it appears there've been interesting developments in the last few weeks. You made a statement saying you had absolutely no intention of going back on your plan for providing housing on the site, but then just a week after that there is a secret meeting between you and two civil servants from the Department of the Environment . . .

Geal Untrue. Untrue, untrue.

He is edging his one uneaten sandwich away from **Colin**'s *hand, which is getting terribly near it.*

Colin We have a memo to prove it. (*He smiles.*) Would you believe! Written by A.R.A. with B.G. – I take it that's you – and B.F. present. It says 'meeting with Lappenshaw Mercantile about whether they will be held to promises – '

Geal How did you get hold of this? This is just 'let's get the wicked developers', standard knocking stuff.

Colin (*effortlessly*) We don't think you're wicked, just seeing what you can get away with, like everyone.

Geal This is all untrue. I question the authenticity of this document. Let me –

Colin *wheels himself out of range.*

Colin No, no, gentlemen, don't be so eager, you will see it all in due course when we publish it in five days. Now I think you should just listen. (**Geal** *edging his sandwich almost into safety along the table –* **Colin** *wheels himself right up to desk, staring at him with a sharp grin.*) You are getting a sneak preview of it, before it becomes public. (*Picks up* **Geal**'s *sandwich and sinks his teeth deep into it.*) I think that's very generous of us, don't you Richard? (*Mouth full of sandwich.*)

Richard Oh yes indeed.

Colin Very considerate of us. (*With sandwich.*) Is it curried tuna? I think it is. (*Pushing sandwich up to* **Geal**'s *mouth.*) Have a taste, see what you think. (**Geal** *looks astonished, terrified of the sandwich now* **Colin** *has touched it.*)

Interior: Developer's building passage and lifts: Day:

Colin *in wheelchair and* **Richard** *waiting by lifts, cleaning woman picking up paper cups strewn along passage.*

Colin (*ironic smile, looking at mess*) They're so proud of this building!

Richard Yes. (*Looking at* **Colin**.) That was great.

Colin Yes, the sandwich was nice anyway.

Richard I'll get you back then.

Colin Yes. (*His eyes tense and worried for a moment.*) I suppose you better.

*The lift climbs up towards them, **Richard** wheels **Colin** into it. We see **Colin**'s pale face disappear behind the lift doors.*

*Interior: **Richard**'s bedroom: Early morning:*

*Very early morning, **Richard** lying in bed, hot, sweating, restless, his bare arms stretched out. He is staring at photographs of **Natalie** taken at the picnic which he's put on the wall. He's had some of them blown up. **Natalie** looks imperious in some, seductive in others, staring back at **Richard**. He looks at the clock. 3.45 a.m. He looks back into **Natalie**'s eyes.*

Richard (*muttered*) Just go there . . . GO THERE . . .

*Exterior: **Natalie** and **Sinclair**'s house: Morning:*

Richard *approaches the house, through the flowers. Curtains still drawn downstairs. The door opens surprisingly quickly. The* **Maid**'s *sleepy face.*

Richard It is very early I know – (*Unabashed smile.*) I was just passing . . . happened to be in the area.

Maid (*sharply*) We were already up.

*Exterior: **Natalie** and **Sinclair**'s garden: Day:*

Sinclair *appears through the garden, seeing **Richard** standing at the front door.*

Sinclair Natalie's gone out already.

Richard (*startled*) She's not here!

Sinclair (*watching him carefully*) No – she's not. But I am. Come with me.

Sinclair *moves off through the garden towards the river,*
Richard *following.*

Sinclair We're getting ready.

Richard Ready for what?

Sinclair *turns and smiles and moves towards the river.*

Sinclair It's very convenient you being here – because I'm
not going to work this morning. Definitely not.

Richard (*following* **Sinclair** *to the water's edge*) Where are
we going?

*They reach the river. At the bottom of the garden is a sizeable boat.
Its engine running.*

Sinclair Just a little trip. I've hired this for myself. But it's
perfect you should be here.

Richard (*very apprehensive*) I don't like boats, I think I'll –

Sinclair Don't worry. I know absolutely nothing about
boats either. But he does, Fernando does – he comes with
the boat. (*Indicating tall man driving boat.*) You've *got* to
come Richard.

Close-up of **Richard**, *looking very suspicious.*

Exterior: The river: Day:

Cut to broad stretch of the river, a ripe landscape. **Sinclair** *and*
Richard *sitting high on the stern of the boat,* **Sinclair** *in his
straw hat.*

Sinclair Relax – you're here now.

Richard (*very unrelaxed*) Yes.

*Seductive shots of the river bank, the houses, people in their gardens,
a child on a swing, people eating breakfast outside under a parasol,*

a figure in white standing watching them go past, a timeless, evocative feel. And then we cut back to **Sinclair***'s beady eyes.*

Sinclair So Richard, what is the matter with you? – you can tell me . . .

Richard I don't think so, Sinclair.

Sinclair What do you mean?

Richard There's nothing to tell.

Sinclair You turn up suddenly like this! You ring up in the middle of the night! There's something on your mind.

Richard No more than usual.

Sinclair Are you in love?

Richard No.

Sinclair You sound very definite.

Richard Yes, because I'm definitely not in love. Not with anyone.

Sinclair Who is she? Somebody I know?

Richard Sinclair – I assure you there is no one.

Sinclair *smiles. Shot of the bank, the boat moving into unspoilt countryside, rich landscape. A whole cluster of children are suddenly revealed in a field running down to the river, they all have kites. Big Chinese dragon kites. Large kites, small kites, getting ready for some sort of display, running with them, or moving them on the ground.*

Sinclair Other people's children are wonderful, aren't they?

Richard (*watching them*) Yes. Do Natalie and you plan . . . ?

Sinclair Oh yes, some day . . . Natalie doesn't feel ready at the moment, as I'm sure you know. Relax Richard . . .

Richard (*slight smile*) I told you – I hate boats.

Richard *watching* **Sinclair** *suspiciously. The river narrows, the overhanging trees get nearer the boat.*

Sinclair You know dinosaurs roamed this place more than anywhere else in England.

Shot of the receding river as they move.

Sinclair There was a sort of dinosaur rush hour at certain times of day along this river, great herds wading along here. I think that's why there's something dangerous and exotic about Surrey still, isn't there?

Richard (*avoiding* **Sinclair**'*s gaze staring at the view*) So what will remain of our world Sinclair, in a couple of hundred years?

Sinclair We spend too much time thinking about the end of the world!

Long lens shot of the boat moving through narrow part of the river, **Sinclair** *lying back, his hat half tilted over his eyes, watching* **Richard** *beadily.*

Sinclair It's not going to happen . . . today . . . I promise you. Not before we've had lunch. I'm a professional forecaster remember!

Exterior: Bank of river: Boat moored: Day:

Sinclair (*moving up a little path with hamper*) Come on, I know a secluded spot.

Richard Secluded spot! (*He glances at Fernando.*)

Sinclair Fernando will stay here, he prefers eating on his own.

Richard I'm sure Fernando would love to join –

Sinclair *moving up ahead. Fernando looking down at* **Richard**. **Richard** *smiles at him.*

Richard Is he going to kill me? Do you think?

We cut to a small lake full of lilies, old trees bending over the water, dense foliage, some junk floating among the lilies, but rich almost tropical atmosphere. **Richard** *and* **Sinclair** *on the bank, a white umbrella shielding them.*

Sinclair (*opening the hamper*) You can have anything but the lychees.

Richard (*staring at the bulging hamper*) You didn't know I was coming? You *couldn't* have.

Sinclair No. Of course not.

Richard (*staring at food*) So this was *all* for you?

Sinclair Sure. Why not? (*Staring at lake.*) Probably full of corpses. (*He turns suddenly to* **Richard**.) She's having an affair isn't she?

Richard If you mean Natalie . . .

Sinclair (*peeling lychees*) Who else would I mean! Don't give me dumb replies, please Richard. It insults both of us.

Richard If you mean Natalie. (*He breathes deeply.*) I'm sure Natalie isn't.

The still water, the lilies, the heavy, hot atmosphere.

Sinclair She's lying to me, all the time. When people lie to you, you suddenly can't think about anything else.

Richard (*quiet*) You've spotted little signs have you?

Sinclair Little signs! No, I didn't have to – she's been carrying a giant placard around with her saying 'I'm fucking somebody else'.

Richard (*staring at him, and then flicking a stone into lake*) So who is it?

Sinclair You tell me.

Richard I don't know.

Sinclair I don't believe that.

Richard Sinclair . . . I promise she hasn't talked to me about it. (*Pause. They stare at each other.*)

Sinclair You know I'll find out.

Richard Yes . . . I know.

Sinclair (*chucking stone into lake*) I have a plan now, anyway.

Richard You have?

Sinclair Oh yes. (*Pause.*)

Sound of roaring among the trees, getting louder and louder.
Richard *looks towards the noise with a flicker of alarm. The roaring gets louder still, through the thick foliage he glimpses a large eye, the eye of a creature, a great head. It is moving among the foliage, mysteriously roaming, then it gets bigger. And it erupts out of the bushes. It is revealed as the head of a kite, a dragon kite, more fierce and reptilian than a Chinese dragon. Three children are running with it, they whoop down the opposite bank of the lake, laughing, running and giggling.*

Sinclair (*laughs*) They must have known you were here Richard! Tracked you down.

The children shaking the kite's great head at them and laughing.

Exterior: River: Approaching house: Day:

Shot approaching the back of the house as the boat returns. **Natalie** *is standing in the garden watching them come back,* **Richard**'s *eyes and* **Natalie**'s *meet.*

Interior: The kitchen: Day:

Richard *coming into the kitchen, there are flowers everywhere, the place is heavy with lilies and other flowers. Vases being prepared,* **Natalie** *amongst the flowers.*

Natalie (*strong*) What on earth are you doing here?

Richard A surprise visit. I had to see you.

Natalie We'd agreed –

Richard I don't care what we'd agreed – (*Touching the flowers.*) What's going on here?

Natalie We're leaving –

Richard Leaving? What do you mean?

Natalie And I want the house to look nice for the last weeks we spend in it.

Richard Where are you going?

Sinclair (*suddenly appearing*) America – we're going to live there, in Connecticut.

Richard (*quiet, very startled*) What you mean live?

Sinclair (*breezily*) *Live*, you know – take up residence, change of scene.

Natalie For a few years or so.

Sinclair (*opening cupboard, sorting things*) Yes, this time I had to say yes. I've had many offers before of course – in my line of work it can't be avoided. But this was suddenly irresistible, and we succumbed, didn't we? It wasn't just the money; the house, the timing, everything seemed right.

Sound changing, dialogue fading. We stay on **Richard**, *his preoccupied face, he is stunned by the news. He moves among the lilies.*

Richard (*moving up to* **Natalie**, *who's been saying something to*

Sinclair) We've got to talk about this – (*He tries to move her.*)we have to –

Natalie Of course. (*Half whispers.*) But, but nothing can change, you do understand.

Sinclair (*going through cupboard*) There may be some things for you Richard, if you want. We can't possibly take everything – *Richard* are you listening, are you with us?

Richard looks up, *totally preoccupied.*

Richard (*quiet*) No.

Interior: Hotel lobby: Day:

Tracking shot moving at steady pace across the great expanse of a richly decorated old hotel lobby. **Natalie** *standing looking very smart against the white walls. People moving around her, and having tea in pools of sunlight in chintz armchairs. The genteel clink of china.*

Richard *moving up to her, as she stands looking controlled and elegant.*

Richard We can't talk here – this is ridiculous.

Natalie Can't we?

Natalie *glances around, a group of glacial looking women move past.*

Natalie People having tea. They can't hear.

Richard Why are we out here? You're expecting me to cause trouble are you?

Natalie (*slight smile*) Oh yes.

Richard's *face very close to* **Natalie**, *brushing her cheek.*

Richard (*strong*) We're going somewhere else.

Natalie No. Keep still. *Still.*

She produces a tie, starts to tie it round his neck, her mood febrile but quite happy, becoming a sister again, not sensing the extent of **Richard***'s intensity.*

Richard What's this for?

Natalie I'm meeting Sinclair here in a little while by the way. You can't go in without a tie. They won't let you in without this, *keep still.* (*She smiles.*) Promise me you'll behave yourself.

Interior: The tea rooms: Day:

The old ladies at tables – the main dining room of the hotel with a great glass roof, like the Waldorf. A pianist tinkling on the piano, cucumber sandwiches on the table, **Richard** *and* **Natalie** *opposite each other. All around them elderly couples, especially women, having tea, bobbing hats, afternoon conversations buzzing, gossiping.*

Richard Is it because of me?

Natalie *No.* It's time for a change. Sinclair wants to get out of England, the economy's going down the chute, the atmosphere's getting ugly, and working in an employment agency is not exactly the answer to my dreams. It's a good time to make a move – it's *our* decision.

Richard (*mocking*) '*Our*' decision?

Natalie Yes, it has nothing to do with getting away from you.

Richard *You're* running away now.

Natalie No – it makes sense. Sinclair's a wise man, he is a little over-whelming and maybe I thought I couldn't cope, but I love him and he's right.

Old ladies twitching in their hats, sitting surrounding their table, **Natalie** *watching them.*

Natalie If *they* knew . . . about us.

Richard You find that idea exciting, don't you?

Natalie Not particularly. (*She flicks his hand affectionately.*) But if they knew, they would be surprised. (*Warm smile.*) That's true, isn't it?

Natalie *eating the sandwiches.*

Richard You broke the rules.

Natalie What rules? There were no rules.

Richard I did everything you asked.

Natalie There was no agreement between us, Richard, you know that, my love. (*Casually reaching for another sandwich.*) You can always visit, pop across.

Richard Pop across?

Natalie The ocean. I want you so much as a friend still.

Richard Still?

Richard *is looking down at the table, he seems near to tears.*

Natalie (*not taking this too seriously, warm*) What is this? Richard, come on . . .

Richard I'm asking you very simply, please, don't go yet. I've helped you constantly, after all. So many times. Gave you advice, *which you took*, got you out of depression. Please do this for me.

Natalie (*affectionately*) Look at you – come on, Richard. (*Gently, lightly.*) My love. What's happened. Just lost your inner confidence a little bit . . . that's all. Mid-life crisis at thirty! (*She smiles.*) Maybe they're getting earlier and earlier . . . Come on. (*Knowing smile.*) You could do anything if you put your mind to it. You know that.

Richard (*not looking up*) I'll ask you one more time. (*Powerfully.*) Please.

He looks up, tears are streaming down his face, the pianist picking out a twinkling tune, the old ladies munching sandwiches glancing in surprise, atmosphere of unease spreading across the tea rooms, music jauntily continuing.

Natalie (*calmly*) I should never have let it happen.

She then softens, leans towards **Richard** *sisterly, taking his wrist.*

Richard (*pushing her away*) Stop it –

Natalie (*firm*) I don't believe you're this hooked, you're trying to turn it into some fantasy of your own – this is self-dramatisation.

Richard *still crying, the tears pouring.*

Natalie It's not *that* serious, Richard. (*Touching him.*) This is my beautiful brother here . . . who was funny and not afraid of anything. Just let it go, Richard. (*Touching his hand.*) I've managed it, you can do it, I know you can.

Richard*'s tears have stopped. The pianist playing, old ladies watching.*

Richard That won't happen. I'm not going to let you go away.

Natalie Oh really? So how you going to stop me?

Richard I *will* stop – and you're not safe here. (*Dangerous.*) You thought you could handle me here – but you were wrong.

Sinclair *is by the table, staring down at them.*

Sinclair Hello, you two. You didn't say Richard would be here as well.

Richard *looks down at table, to mask his red face.*

Sinclair English tea, I'm really going to miss these,

cucumber sandwiches, maybe the last ones we'll see for a while.

Interior: Lobby: Day:

Sinclair *and* **Richard** *stand next to each other,* **Porter** *eyeing them,* **Richard** *blowing his nose, turning away from* **Sinclair**.

Natalie Just got to phone work – check on a couple of things.

Sinclair (*watching* **Natalie** *go*) We're having a great time being lazy, saying goodbye to London, going to shows, and to tourist attractions we'd never seen! (*Sharp smile.*) Keeps Natalie occupied. (*He indicates hotel noticeboard.*) These noticeboards are often surprisingly interesting, you can see what's going on elsewhere in the hotel – conference for Cable TV, you see, meeting of FAX manufacturers, share-holders' meeting, all kinds of boardroom struggles going on in this genteel place.

As **Sinclair** *is saying this,* **Richard** *moving away, towards* **Natalie** *in phone booth, he pushes into booth startling* **Natalie**.

Richard (*very strong*) Natalie, I promise, I'm not kidding, you cannot go.

Natalie *holding phone,* **Richard** *pressed up to her.*

Natalie Get out of here!

Close-up of **Richard**.

Natalie Richard, I told you, there's no going back.

Richard I can't answer for what will happen – if you do try to leave.

Natalie Stop being so melodramatic – you're determined to make something happen –

Richard (*holding her, kissing the side of her face*) This is *me*

Natalie. You know I'm never desperate about anything. I never expected this to happen, either. BUT IT HAS. Come with me . . . Just to talk. Get rid of Sinclair. Come to my flat! You know. *You've got to.* You must.

Porter *knocking on glass*, **Natalie** *twisting her head round, manages to open door.*

Porter Is the lady all right?

Natalie Yes – this is only my brother. (*She moves off, furious whisper to* **Richard**.) For Chrissake – stop it.

They emerge out of phone booth, **Porter** *watching them.* **Sinclair** *is at end of the corridor.*

Sinclair What on earth happened? Where did you go?

Richard (*calling*) She just wanted some change.
(*Whispered.*) You *will* come Natalie. By 5.30. You must.

Natalie *moving off.*

I'm waiting for you.

Interior: **Richard**'s *room: Day:*

Richard *alone, the clock showing it's 6.20, golden evening light.*

Noise of somebody on the stairs. Close-up of **Richard**. *They pass his door and go up.* **Richard**'s *face very tense and determined..*

Richard Jesus – how did this happen?

Interior: **Richard**'s *bathroom: Day:*

Richard *goes into the bathroom. Very casually and haphazardly he starts taking all the pills that are there. We see bottle of sleeping pills. He takes everything in the bathroom, pouring them down his*

*throat, very matter-of-fact. They all go down. Empty bottles
clinking into the bath.*

Exterior: Building site: Day:

We cut to **Richard** *wandering down into the great building site,
the dust, the machines, the great hole in the ground, moving among
the workmen, a hallucinatory feeling, the plastic sheeting swirling,
men in goggles staring at him, scaffolding moving overhead, people
looking at him strangely, the cranes towering into the sky. He
wanders further and further into the site, the sounds getting
distorted, the images more vivid, enveloping him, the tremendous size
of the site and* **Richard** *in the middle of it.*

Interior: **Richard**'s *bedroom: Day:*

Cut to **Richard**'s *face hitting his pillow. His eyes closing, his
face strange. His eyes flicker open. Then his body is wracked with
vomiting, his body spinning over, off bed.*

Natalie *is standing over him, pulling him up.*

Natalie (*calm*) Come on, come here. (*Pulling him toward the
bathroom.*)

Interior: **Richard**'s *bathroom: Day:*

Natalie *holds* **Richard** *as he retches.*

Natalie Silly boy, you took vitamin pills as well, more
vitamin pills than sleeping pills it looks like. (*Affectionate
smile, touching him.*) Not the best way to kill yourself.

Interior: **Richard**'s *bedroom: Day:*

Cut to **Richard** *curled up on bed.* **Natalie** *stroking his hair. It is dark now.*

Natalie I came back for the tie actually. (*Smiles.*) Partly for that.

He is still wearing it. She takes it off.

Natalie It's rather a good one. You've messed it up. (*Stroking his hair.*) You wanted to frighten me, did you? You half managed it. (*Calm.*) You're precious to me Richard, don't want you to hurt yourself, but I'm not going to let you destroy us both. Come on pull yourself together – I don't love you when you look like this, all messy and –

Richard (*quiet*) Please, whatever you do, don't tell me to pull myself together.

Natalie OK, OK . . . now if you behave yourself, and if you're brave enough – you can come to our going away party, do you want to do that?

Richard (*looking at her*) I'll see Natalie.

Natalie (*staring invitingly from door*) I think you'll manage it somehow.

Interior: 'Urban Alert' offices: Day:

Office empty except for **Jessica** *and* **Richard**. *Three others including the pudgy girl just leaving for the day.* **Jessica** *is wearing black.* **Richard** *watching her across the whole expanse of the big office.*

Colin's *belongings, his clothes, several pairs of shoes and socks are in neat stacks on a table in the corner. The inky thriller is staring back at* **Richard**.

Jessica Stop staring at them – they'll be going soon.

Richard It's OK – I don't mind. (*He can't keep his eyes off them.*) I think we should keep them here. In memory.

Jessica (*warm smile*) You don't sound too sure.

Richard (*very firm*) No. I am. We should.

Richard *watching* **Jessica**, *formidable behind her desk.*

Richard You'll do well, running this place.

Jessica (*slight smile*) High praise. Thank you.

Richard Come with me tomorrow, please.

Exterior: Gardens of large house near river: Day:

The formal gardens of a house, like Ham House, near river. **Sinclair** *and* **Natalie** *have hired a part of the gardens for their farewell party. Groups of people in summer dresses,* **Philippa** *looking beautiful with her children. Champagne and food, a band in red and white playing on gold banqueting chairs on the grass, a microphone on a platform by a summer house, a rich valedictory atmosphere.*

Sinclair *in his element, moving round, joking with people, dazzling people. He takes the microphone.*

Sinclair Just to say the food is not being eaten with sufficient ferocity. There'll be no speeches of any kind, but quite often I will be grabbing the microphone to urge you to eat and drink. *Also* anything that you've been longing to say to us for years and felt you never could, *now* is the time, don't hold back, anything that is insulting, shocking, spiteful, gross, this is turning itself into a speech, definitely forcing itself into a speech, so the only way to stop myself –

Sinclair *walks sharply away from the mike in mid-sentence.*

Richard *and* **Jessica** *together moving among the Surrey people* *and the formal gardens.* **Richard** *staring at* **Natalie** *and* **Sinclair** *conducting the party.*

Richard Look at them, they are like presiding royalty, saying goodbye and good riddance to all of us.

Jessica Why do you mind so much?

Richard *watching* **Natalie** *all the time. In a series of stronger and stronger images he sees* **Natalie** *with* **Sinclair**. *She's teasing him, ordering him about, behaving with a real confidence with him, effortless and relaxed.*

Natalie (*teasing* **Sinclair** *in front of others*) No he's hopeless with modern appliances – trust a business analyst to be helpless with machines! (*Moving with* **Sinclair** *through party.*) No, you've never seen Sinclair's table manners! They are X certificate – frighten children off eating for days. (*She laughs, touching* **Sinclair**.) He loves being teased.

Richard *watching her, her confidence. She turns and stares at him, gives him a seemingly secret look, a look saying 'it is over', then turns away back to friends.*

Exterior: Edge of garden/road near party: Day:

Richard *filling with fury. He follows her round the party, watches her all the time. Suddenly grabs her when she is for a moment on the edge of the party, pulling her away, through the grass and trees, further and further from the guests.*

Natalie (*shouts, yelling*) Stop it Richard – what are you doing? Please – please, stop it.

Richard God, I want to kill you, you know that?

He pulls her through the apple trees, as she yells and shouts, trying to fight him off.

Richard It's so easy for you. *Easy.* I hate you.

They come out of the trees, rolling down a bank of grass on top of each other, onto a narrow road. They lie in the middle of the long straight road. **Richard** *on top of her, pulling her arms back.*

Richard You used me – didn't you.

Natalie (*fighting back*) Used you.

Richard To get a little excitement into your marriage, make it take fire again – make you feel strong, (*Strange, mocking.*) help you 'find yourself' – a little bored were you in your wonderful house – just play with this shall we – (*Strange, mocking.*) now we're all refreshed again, are we!

Natalie Richard, please.

Richard And now you think, no longer need him, let's throw him away – WHAT ABOUT ME? WHAT HAS HAPPENED TO ME? I hate you . . . I *won't* allow you to . . .

Natalie (*furious*) Stop this Richard, I'm warning you, I'm warning . . .

Richard (*twisting* **Natalie***'s head around*) What if you were pregnant?

Natalie But I'm not. (*Strong.*) I'm not . . .

Richard The child would have an enormous head probably, wouldn't it! . . .

Natalie Richard – you're going to stop this.

A lorry nearly mows them down as they fight, rolling out of its path. A cathartic fight, **Richard***'s rage pouring over her,* **Natalie** *is crying, fighting him away, tears roll down her,* **Richard** *begins to stop, they both collapse onto each other, exhausted and bleeding.*

They lie on top of each other by the road, oblivious of any passing cars.

Natalie (*touching him, curling his hair*) I'm sorry . . . I didn't mean to use you . . . maybe I did use you. (*Running her fingers down his nose.*) Now we're even.

Richard Are we? (*Pause.*)

Natalie I love you . . . (*Lightly.*) I knew you'd want this to end with one of us dying, trust you to get both of us nearly killed.

A car full of daytrippers, passing this strange couple on top of each other.

Natalie I'll tell you a secret . . .

Richard What secret?

Natalie Is it over? Not going to erupt again?

Richard Not for the moment. What is it?

Natalie We're not going away, Sinclair's deal fell through. But we still wanted to have the party.

Richard, *slight smile.*

Natalie Serves me right doesn't it.

Exterior: Gardens of house: Day:

We cut back to the party. The evening light. Slowly on the edge of the frame **Natalie** *and* **Richard** *move towards us, badly cut from the road, bedraggled, their clothes torn, but they move nonchalantly through the guests, who part in front of them, looking startled, forming a path for them, as the guests back away.*

Richard *and* **Natalie** *sit down at a table – the white tablecloth flapping.* **Sinclair** *staring at them.* **Natalie** *casually pours herself an orange juice.* **Sinclair** *moves up to the table.*

Sinclair Something tells me it's the end of the party.

Sinclair *sits, staring from* **Natalie** *to* **Richard** *and back. People watching all three of them as they sit at the table.* **Jessica**

looking very startled. Bewildered guests begin to melt away. The musicians play on, as the party empties. Till only the three and the musicians are left.

Interior: **Sinclair** *and* **Natalie***'s house: Sitting room: Day:*

We see **Sinclair** *alone, staring into a mirror, deeply pensive, trying to retain control, quietly stunned.*

Interior: **Sinclair** *and* **Natalie***'s house: Evening:*

Natalie *lying on sofa in hallway.* **Sinclair** *gently wiping cream on her legs, and folding a bandage.* **Richard** *is sitting watching,* **Natalie***'s eyes half closed. A late summer evening, sound of woodpigeons, dreamy, quiet.*

Sinclair Does that feel all right?

Natalie (*quiet*) Yes.

Sinclair You look like you've been in mortar fire you two.

Natalie (*lying in profile*) We have.

Richard You know don't you – you know everything.

Sinclair Know what?

Richard About me and Natalie.

Sinclair (*simply*) I know a few things, I know there was something extraordinary between you two, something that had to be purged. (*Holds up his hand in case* **Richard** *tells him more,* **Sinclair***'s face pale but controlled.*) I don't want to know any more, there is a limit beyond which I can't go, I don't want to hear. (*Slight pause.*) It's enough that the worst is over.

Richard (*quiet*) You think so?

Sinclair Yes. I believe that – yes. (*Staring at* **Richard**.) Getting less intense . . . isn't it?

Richard (*quiet*) You're being so . . . calm Sinclair. It's amazing.

Sinclair I'm amazed myself. Somebody had to be calm around here. (*Self-mocking smile, pause.*) I mean I could start screaming . . . maybe I will. Delayed shock. Who knows? . . . (*Quiet.*) *I don't think so.* I hope not.

Natalie (*half opens her eyes, warm*) I told you he was wise, didn't I.

Richard (*quiet*) So Sinclair – you know everything. (*Pause, the sounds of the summer evening.*) What's going to happen then?

Sinclair To us or the human race?

Richard (*lightly*) Both.

Sinclair (*pause*) I haven't a clue.

Exterior: River: Evening:

They are walking along the river bank, the three of them, dusk just falling. A couple of bonfires in people's gardens sending smoke across the water and into the evening sky.

They walk away from the camera.

Sinclair Bonfires! Look. That's autumn! (*Looks across at bonfires, the smoke wafting.*) Those fires, always the typical English end to summer.

Natalie (*gently*) I certainly wouldn't call this summer typical . . .

Richard (*pulling at the leaves by the river, quiet*) No . . .

They move on along the bank.

Sinclair (*glancing at the river*) It could be a good idea we're not going away after all. (*Waves at the view.*) I might have begun to miss this.

They move away from us along the river. Slowly a wipe starts at the top of the screen, turning the final image into a drawing, catching them there, in the distance on the river bank, as they have instantaneously moved into the past, and this summer has already become a memory, of the early nineties.